Reach down grab your pair AND START LIVING!

By: Trev2323

Printed in the United States of America.
For information or inquiries:
Robert Trevino
P.O. Box 712,
Dolton, Il. 60419

ISBN: 978-1-257-97935-6

FIRST EDITION
Text Design: Robert & Leanne M. Trevino

Cover Design: G. Velez

This book is written with the support of my beautiful wife
who I sincerely thank for standing by my side
through thick and thin
and the ups and downs.
I love you

**A wise man once told me “you can choose your emotions,
you can choose to be happy or you can choose to be mad, either way the choice is yours"**

This one little phrase has changed the way I live my life from that day forward.

INSTRUCTIONS

This book is not meant to be read straight through as fast as you can!

Read one chapter at least 3 times and do not move on to the next chapter until you feel as if you completely understand and duplicated the last chapter you read.

Knowledge does not equal power, APPLIED knowledge does.

CONTENTS

Prelude

I guess this prelude is supposed be a little bit about myself. Growing up in life I was always entrepreneurial minded and never wanted to work for somebody my entire life. I've always searched a never-ending life quest for other ways and other means of bringing a little more income so I can retire at an earlier age. In this quest of trying so many different opportunities I stumbled upon many different points of interest that I believe, in general, an abundance of men may be interested in. I.e. the adult world, relationships with the opposite sex, party like a rock star, and just living life to the fullest.

I always had my one career which was my stable career for the insurance of my kids. But I always knew working for somebody else would never make me rich so I always strive for more in life. Some tell me I have the gift of gab but I wasn't born with it. I'd venture to say my gift of gab and being able talk to anybody was my form of my own little Napoleon syndrome. Instead of being all feisty aggressive physically, I was more or less feisty and aggressive in talking to everybody and I don't mean aggressive as "aggressive"I mean as aggressive as you going up to people and being able talk to people.

So where did this all come together with the book? Well I traveled the world of serving in the Armed Forces, worked in various forms of marketing, and owned various types of adult businesses. Anywhere I went guys desired to talk to more ladies, be surrounded by more ladies, and party like all fucking rock stars.

Now if you put this into business terms, either way it goes you still need to get out there and talk to more people. Sometimes people want to climb the corporate ladder, but normally when you climb a ladder you're only looking at one rum above to put your hand. Maybe you should stop, sit back and look at the top of the building and make sure that your ladder is up against the building you want it to be and you're sure that's the ladder you would like to climb.

I wrote this book for the guys who desire a change in life, the guys who feel that they're introverts and would like to experience being a extrovert. To this day when I go out I see a bunch of guys, guys that go out to meet girls but yet don't say anything to a lady when they're out. On the other hand you see groups of ladies standing together moving around to the beat of the music all dolled up waiting for somebody to ask them to dance and yet nobody does.

This book isn't just for the "nerds" in life because there are many "nerds" in life that have beautiful ladies on their arms experiencing life to the fullest. I guess you could say this book is just for the people who desire more out of life. Any chapter that you read you can apply towards your current life, in a nutshell the book is for people who desire a lot more of life and I have hopes to help you achieve it.

I wrote this book in a way you could understand it as I would understand it. The book is more or less like me, short and to the point. I don't have lengthy fluff words throughout the book to stretch out longer. I have information and food for thought for you to read it, get through it and take some action. There are some life experiences I've been through after some of the chapters.

You can skip past them if you just want the motivation and self help that I'm trying to provide.

One thing I've learned in life is that nothing is a failure if you learn from it and grow. I also relate that to if you purchase something, book, audio, video, and you learned one thing from it it was worth it. So I'm hoping that you learn at least one thing out of this book. But with that one thing put into action and keep striving for what you truly desire in life.

DESIRE, DESIRE, DESIRE

Who in life never desires something? One thing we are born with is the emotion desire (some people say Satan puts it in us). I feel this is a great emotion that controls our subliminal mind and has a fucking huge impact in our ultimate destiny. We wouldn't even be here if Adam didn't desire Eve in the beginning.

Since the time we were little kids we had a desire for something in life. From that kick ass BMX bike you wanted, to the latest hot rod you wanted, to the fucking hot ass teacher that taught in your grammar school or high school there was a desire. The crazy thing is that a lot of us desire for things in life, things that are very tangible and achievable yet we don't pursue them because for some reason we kill our own dreams. We either feel she's out of my league... or I can never have that. Fuck, who would of EVER thought Vince Vaughn would of ever hooked up with Jennifer Aniston? BUT he did! He desired her and had the balls to pursue her and ran away with the gold medal.

Heck I know you and I both would of loved the chance to be with her little fine ass.

So why don't you pursue something you have always desired in life? Think about it... Really right now.. Stop reading, put the book down and fucking think about one thing, take baby steps if you need to but think of just one thing that you truly desire in life. It can be from something as simple as right now I desire a candy bar, to I really desire a nice hot piece of ass right now.. to right now you desire a new career or maybe a different car, but seriously stop and think about it... Did you come up with something? If you didn't close this book and give it to someone who wants more out of life and keep going through the life that you currently have. If you did come up with something, what was it? REALLY? I'm asking! If you're alone say it out loud, if not think about whatever it is right now with extreme passion. FEEL IT! Sounds crazy but say out loud and ask the universe to give you the knowledge, skills and ability to get whatever it is that you are desiring in life right now. The universe is way bigger than all of us and usually will give you all the means to get what you desire in life. The emotion desire can play with your mind weekly, daily, hourly even every second of the day. But if you don't put any action towards it you will never get it. It will only remain a desire.

You now have to figure out what the fuck you have to to do to get it. The desire is the first step in the equation but an important one that has to remain there for the duration until you get exactly what you want and beyond.

This may sound crazy but when I used to work out I would have pictures of fine ass ladies all around the room. Bikini pictures from Maxim magazine, Hustler, FHM, and Low Rider magazine. The average guy who works out has pictures of muscle men all around, the Lou Ferrigno and Arnold Schwarzenegger Mr Olympias. These are what they are desiring to look like. I had my pictures up because those were the ladies I desired to be with, therefore those types of pictures motivated me more to work out. I worked out to those pictures because I wanted to be in shape to get me some sweet delicious ass.

SO remember we can get whatever we desire in life BUT we have to put ACTION towards getting what we desire. You have to stop feeling sorry for yourself and stop doubting yourself. YOU CAN GET IT, YOU DESERVE IT! If you whole heart-idly desire it enough and put at least 10% of your day towards it you can achieve it.

Ten percent of your day isn't a lot at all. Think about all the days in your life that have come and gone already and you haven't made any efforts towards your dreams, desires or goals.

Your desire for complacency and laziness has been greater than your desire for change, then your desire for greatness, your desire for financial freedom, a new companion or even just a piece of ass. If I'm wrong tell me, No tell yourself but this time don't make any excuses CHANGE IT! COMMIT TO MAKING A CHANGE TODAY! RIGHT NOW! Think about it in your mind right now, what you truly desire. Go ahead dust off them dreams that for some reason you put to the side, or felt you couldn't achieve them.

Let's do this together as a team, a team of underdogs that will prevail. OWN IT! FEEL IT ! TASTE IT! And don't let anybody steal your thunder. When we finally meet in person and party together I want to hear all about your changes, conquests and results. When you become that proud successful HAPPY stud living life to the fullest. I want you to help spread the word and help other people take life by the balls and live it to the fullest.

By you even choosing to buy or download this book, you are already saying you desire more in life. Well go ahead desire it, dream it and get it. Set some goals and train your subliminal mind to at least 3 times a day concentrate and fantasize about everything you want in life. See yourself achieving all your wildest dreams and goals. See how your life would be once you have achieved them.

Now commit to yourself that you will give at minimum 10% a day and take SOLID steps towards achieving your dreams and goals. Keep the fire going my friend because you have my complete support. I know you and I can achieve greatness together.

So now I need you to GO FOR IT! Take the first step right now. I'm going to show you how your brain can really picture EXTREME DESIRE just by putting clear and concise images in your mind. Picture a beautiful pussy, a nice beautiful shaved pussy... MMM close your eyes, where was the last one you saw? Was it at a strip club? Are you thinking of the last lady you fucked? How about a nice pussy from that beautiful playboy playmate? Picture it? Can you? I love the essence of a pussy, can you smell it? Is your mouth starting to water? Imagine those juices as you're sliding your fingers in and out of it. Do you want it right now?? WELL GET OFF YOUR ASS and do something towards getting you there. Imagine and crystallize exactly what you want in life. SUCCESS, REALTIONSHIPS, HAPPINESS, dream plenty and dream big. NOW GO FINISH THE REST OF THIS BOOK.

This chapter is for the married men

Okay guys now that you have your desire down pact, if you're married let me put you to a screeching halt! This chapter is for the married guys who are desiring to live out their sexual fantasies, this chapter isn't really a business or self-improvement chapter although you may still find it interesting.

I have this conversation with every guy I meet who wants to know more about the wild side in life and dig deeper into living out them sick men sadistic Sodom and Gomorrah fantasies. I ask the men if they're married. If so, before you go on be sure you're ready for the repercussions if you get caught. Some men have the privilege of having an open minded spouse or significant other who will indulge in the complete sexual fantasies with you, but most won't and think that you are a sick fuck. Well yes, I was that sick fuck and I damn near lost everything indulging in the plethora of ladies who were wide open desiring to be filled with as many cocks as they could find.

When I used to own my adult bookstore I used to have guys come in all the time asking if I had viewing booths, or if I knew where the massage parlors were "that the ladies did extra". A lot of the guys asking seemed like well dressed professionals and guys just getting off work.

They were looking for some extra action right when they got out of work or on their day off to relieve some stress before they went home. They figured since I owned an adult bookstore that I knew where all the action was. Well hey they were right, but they didn't expect when I asked them "Are you married? and if so think about what you're doing because where you want to go is very addictive." During the time I had my adult bookstore open there were two adult theaters in the area that had ladies and couples playing in there all the time. There were adult bookstores with glory holes in the viewing booths (glory holes are there for guys to stick their cock through while they're watching a video so the person on the other side could be pleasuring them.)

I would tell them "You have to really sit down and think about this lifestyle"...Is this worth it??? Are these desires worth giving up marriage...family...and the biggest thing that will be thrown in your face-HALF! I'm getting half!! Ha ha ha... Not to bring anyone down or anything but people and feelings get hurt when you start to pursue your sexual desires. **Heck if you're single, wrap that rascal and have at it.**

If you wanna try starting with your wife first... Bring it up to her, what's her fantasies? Or you don't want her to live out hers you just want to live yours? I know plenty of couples where the wife plays harder than the guy and the guy goes along for the wild ride. BUT wait.. If you're one of those guys who has a wife at home who is always pissed or not in the mood then open up that line of communication and figure that shit out. You aren't getting any younger and there are many other ladies out there that will talk, laugh, and joke with you and there are many other guys out there that will make her laugh and talk with her, joke with her oh yea and fuck her brains out. So don't be miserable with one person your whole life if it isn't working. If something isn't working open up that line of communication. DONT ARGUE just straighten out that currently meaningless relationship. Hell if you're married then at one time she found you interesting, laughed at your jokes, sucked your cock and rode you like a mad woman right? Where do you think all that went to? If you wake up and see her every morning and think why the hell am I here? Or what the hell did we do to get here? Then you're waking up every morning not trying to make it work. If you want to work and bring back the romance you have to work at it, be the bigger person and bite that bullet. When you wake up every morning and see your wife or significant other be grateful for the things she does. Change that in your mind. You'll find out that once you change your train of thought that you may start enjoying time with her.

This works for your job also, if you go to work every day and on the way to work all you think is, I hate my job, I hate my job, I hate my job, then guess what, I bet you hate your job. You have to find the little good things that are there at your job. Concentrate on those and focus on those until you finish reading this book and really do what you want to do in life.

Now this isn't a marriage manual I just don't want anyone coming back at me calling me asshole for messing up their marriage. The reality is your spouse has to be a freak and very open minded to party as hard as what is out there **BUT** she may be willing **if you bring it out of her, and yes I did say if you bring it out of her because that is completely possible**. Sex is a very powerful addiction, like cocaine, especially if you find all the nooks and crannies where the cock mongers and the gang bangs are. I mean there are networks and groups where fine pussy is a plenty.

If you never tell a lie in the beginning, you don't ever have to remember what you said. Either way it goes this book is not only for the guys who desire to party like a rock star and bang every lady on the planet. This book is A LOT a**bout stepping out of your comfort zone and becoming a different, more confident person.**

Someone who might take a little more chances in life, do something they may never have experienced in life or if you take it to the EXTREME completely change your life and live out all your dreams.

It's your journey in life, you choose the destination and the vehicle you're using to get there. In my eyes we have to be here and live life anyway so WHY NOT live life to the fullest and have a kick ass time doing it and pursue all you truly desire in life!

Short story: when you get to these parts feel free to skip over them, they're nothing about self-improvement, they're more or less experiences of my life that other guys may want to experience. Well be careful because you think you're on top of the world, but it may be a downward spiral.

One day I was off work and I felt like scraping the bottom of the barrel. There's a little adult dive with a theater about 25 min. from my apartment. You could go online to check to see if there's any action going on in the theater but whether the theater is happening or not there's always ladies lined up for "private dances". So in cruising the net I noticed that there was a couple at the theater so I figured let me cruise on over and maybe check out a live show. Pulling up to the theater or bookstore whatever you want to call it, I see there is like three other cars in the lot and a kick ass Harley-Davidson motorcycle.

It's funny because when you pull up to the store you can sit in your car and look back and forth, up and down the street to see if there's any cars passing by so they don't notice you walking in. I got up to the door and was buzzed in.

Once inside I see there were two ladies in lingerie sitting at the counter but they were regulars who look to get some "private dances" to help pay their bills. At the counter is where you have to pay to get into the theater, so the girls kind of flirt with you as you're waiting to pay to get into the theater.

So I paid my money and walked over to the theater (the theater was actually a little room maybe 12 x 15 completely black no lights except for lights coming off of a 46 inch screen TV.) To my amazement I walked into a couple fucking buck wild right in the first row. Well I found out whose Harley that was, she was riding him reverse cowgirl with nothing on but her leather biker vest. I mean her pussy was spread wide open and her tits were bouncing all over. Her hands were holding on to the theater seat and she was fucking the hell out of him. She was maybe mid-40s, reddish brunette hair and a nice tanned complexion. I'm guessing from riding on the Harley. She had to be maybe between 138 and 148 pounds. Nice body. He looked like an older gentleman. He had to be in his 50s actually and slightly overweight.

I was surprised to see him with her. He had a Harley-Davidson bandanna around his head, his jeans were already around his ankles and he also had a biker vest on.

They were right in the front row and I kind of glanced out of my peripheral vision as I walked by them going to the back row. There was one other guy in the back row at the other end. I didn't even notice him because I was focused on her going crazy.

I didn't even have to watch the show playing on the screen because she was getting more into it than the lady on the screen. After going at it for a bit she got off of his cock and sat in the seat next to him. You could tell from behind she was still stroking his cock. She looked over her shoulders glanced at the guy in the other end and then glanced at me continually stroking his cock and they had a little conversation. She looked back over my way and motioned me over to them. She said "Come on baby sit right here" and she pointed to a seat on the other side of her. Up close there was more light to see she was definitely a MILF. She was still stroking his cock and started rubbing on my cock through my jeans. I started to rub my hand on her inner thigh and she didn't stop me, she actually bent over in the chair and started sucking her man's cock. She was completely bent over the chairs arm with nothing but her biker vest on and I was seeing all her glory. As she was bent over like that I started fingering her from behind. I had one hand on her hips and I had three fingers of my other hand going in and out of her.

She turned around and sat back in the chair so I thought she wasn't feeling me. She asked her man for her purse that was on the other side of him and he grabbed it and gave it to her. She actually pulled out some baby wipes and antibacterial and asked if I minded using it. She poured some in my hands and I started rubbing my hands together. She asked me to stand up in front of her and she undid my belt buckle and my zipper and pulled my pants to my knees. She took out the baby wipes and started stroking my cock and rubbing my balls with the baby wipes.

Hell it felt like a nice oriental massage! She asked if I had any condoms and I said I sure did. She actually asked me what kind they were and I replied “Trojans ribbed and lubed.” She was like “Okay that's cool.” She put everything back in her purse handed it to her man and went right down sucking my cock. He seemed like he was enjoying this very much. He was stroking his cock watching her suck my cock. She didn't want to leave him left out, so she started stroking his cock as she was sucking my cock. After a while of playing like this she went right into the middle between his two legs and started sucking his cock again. So I was like oh okay and she asked if I had a condom so apparently she figured I could play. As she was bent over sucking her man's cock I put my condom on and started fucking her from behind. Her man really loved this! He actually came in her mouth as I was taking her from behind.

He was saying "I have to cum baby I have to cum” she says “Go ahead I'll catch it all” I'll be damned if she didn't miss a drop. I didn't miss a beat, I kept fucking her as he was cumming and they were both getting into it. I figured since he was done it would be all over, but no, I was wrong. I sat in the chair as she jumped on me and started to ride me reverse cowgirl. I was holding on to her tits as she was bouncing up and down and man she was fucking me good. I felt somebody over my shoulder and the other guy in the theater actually moved to the row right behind me. He wanted a closer view and I bet he was pissed she didn't pick him. As she was riding me he was stroking his cock. She seemed as if her thighs were getting tired so I turned around to bend her over the theater seat.

There we were doggy style and she was so good she actually put both her knees on the seat to bend over more so I was given a clear shot fucking the hell out of her. As we're fucking like this her man stood up with his erect cock still stroking it and asked me "Could I get some of that right now" I sure hoped he was talking about his lady because he sure wasn't getting any of me. I pulled my cock out of her and sat in the theater seat a couple of chairs down and he shoved his cock in her and started fucking her again. I wasn't even sitting down for a minute and she told me to go in the other aisle and stand behind the theater seat so she could suck my cock as he was fucking her. There we three were sweating our asses off and we had the other guy in there just watching. If I were that other guy I would've been stroking my cock watching the show. The next act took me by surprise, he sat back down in the theater chair and she stopped sucking my cock and sat on him to ride his cock regular cowgirl style. She motioned me to come back around the other side so by this time there was just my shirt on, and I couldn't believe what came out of her mouth. She said "Stick your cock in my ass" I didn't believe I heard her right. She must have seen me with a dumbfounded look and said again "Stick your cock in my ass and fuck me" Before I did that I took my condom off and threw it in the makeshift garbage can they had there. I put a fresh condom on and and stuck my cock right in her ass. I went slow, I wasn't a complete asshole, but she wanted a DP and her man was going to allow her to have it. So there I was not knowing who the hell either of these people were. She was a superfine MILF and he looked like a Harley riding Santa Claus, but I have to give it to the man because he kept his cock hard for a long time for her.

He was still going strong but of course this was his second nut he was building up, and I on the other hand felt like cumming so quick because I couldn't believe that this superfine biker chick had me in her tight asshole. So I said “Okay I'm ready, it's my turn, I have to cum now”, and she said “Go ahead baby leave it in my ass, I want to feel your cock throbbing as you're cumming.” Believe me she didn't have to tell me twice. I filled up that condom so full I had cum dripping down my balls. When I finished I pulled out and they kept going for a little while longer. I took my condom off and threw it in the garbage. The theater was always nice enough to have a roll of paper towels in the back.

When she saw me go for the paper towels she said “Don't worry baby I have some stuff we could clean up with”. She again brought out her antibacterial along with her baby wipes and she actually cleaned me off with the baby wipes again and she did a really good job. They asked if I come there often, and I told them once in a while. They told me thank you very much for the good time and they hoped to see me again. Unfortunately this was the first and only time I ever met up with this couple. But they're still out there and if you get your butt out there and start talking to some people maybe you'll bump into them or somebody like them. If you don't get out there and don't start talking to people and don't start living life and having a good time, then someone else will! So get out there and have a great time!

Stop being a lump on a log

One of my big pet peeves in life are the people who want to do a lot more things in life yet never go out at all PERIOD! Getting out is actually being Pro active in life. I mean yes you can meet people in cyber world, BUT REAL LIFE to me is more fun.

When ever you're out it gives you a chance to practice talking to people. As you go out more often you will find yourself getting invited to more parties and events by the more people you meet…. As long as you're not an obnoxious asshole.

Do you talk to people at work? And I'm not talking about your X box friends or Trekkie friends. I'm talking about people of the opposite sex. Everywhere you go you should practice talking to ladies, EVERYWHERE! Strike up small conversations in line at the grocery stores, while pumping gas, playing your lottery tickets, there is another human being standing right there to practice your conversation skills on. Make sure while you're going out whether its relationships, dates, prospects, or whatever you're looking for that you are clean, have nice shoes on (for some fucking reason ladies pay VERY close attention to guys shoes) and I believe in good, no in great smelling cologne. So instead of buying the new freaky alien killers game for X box or dropping more money on slutty amateur auditions #1003 go buy some excellent smelling cologne.

You know a great conversation starter is actually asking ladies what kind of cologne they like. Don’t forget be clean and tight not a wrinkle bomb and start a conversation like “ Excuse me I am thinking on changing up my cologne and was wondering if there is any particular kind of cologne you like? Or maybe your friends may have mentioned one?” If they answer with a name brand you can follow that up with “ Do you know where I can get it at? “. Here is another follow up question “If you can think back is there a particular type of cologne that your boyfriend or an ex wears or used to wear?” This same conversation can be duplicated on co-workers, ladies that work at the cologne stations in the stores, ladies in line at the grocery stores, man I mean ladies you meet anywhere, BUT if you don't get out you’ll never be able to talk to them. The more people you begin to meet the more you’ll be invited out and you really need to go to whatever it is you’re invited to. Like child birthday parties – guess what? There will be other moms there and a great chance to practice your conversation skills. Want to stand out? Buy a kick ass gift for the birthday child, look nice and smell good (and not too much where you smell like a French whore). Mingle, mingle, mingle. Work the room and small talk with everyone at the party. Be quirky, not obnoxious. You may find out that there will be someone there at the party that you may have something in common with. The more parties you go to with the same friends the more you’ll meet up with the same people and start to build relationships.

There have been guys that I have met up with at gang bangs (YES I SAID GANG BANGS) (gang bangs with real ladies) and we started hanging out together. They would call me if they had a lady who desired to be gang banged and I would call them if I knew of any gang bangs going on. Now don't plan on meeting these kinds of ladies at the kid's birthday parties but you may be surprised what they may turn into when their not being mom. I hope your getting the drift "TAP ROOT" keep meeting, talking, making friends, and meet their friends. Get to know everyone. Meet people at parties and ask " So how do you know so and so?" " Well I know them from_____" "Yea I think he or she is good people" " How long have you known them?" " WANNA FUCK?" HA HA HA just kidding "Are you from around here?" "Do you know of any bars or clubs around here?" I like getting out and trying new or exciting places.

So if you get invited to anything you must go! Every party, birthday, retirement, or even a shopping trip is a entirely new opportunity to talk to someone new. Yes reach down grab your pair and start talking.

Heck if you mess this conversation up guess what? There are billions of people in this world to practice on so just keep learning from your mistakes and keep practicing and eventually someone will let you suck on their tits and maybe even fuck them. Just remember be clean, smell good, make them laugh and show them a good time.

Hell I have been to gang bangs and at some of them you didn't have to do anything at all just show up. These ladies didn't want any conversations, just cocks and plenty of them.

So why aren't you going out more often? Nowhere to go? Nothing to wear? No way to get there?? All of these are excuses. If you want to change your life you have to EXTREMELY DESIRE the change. You have to desire it ten times more than the FEAR that's holding you back from the change. So get off your ass right now and get out there into the game of life. The time it took you to read this chapter you can never get back in life. That time is gone. Don't let anymore time pass you by.

Short Story: One day I was off work and kind of lazy to tell you the truth, I was sitting on the couch at my bachelor apartment all by myself. I was bored out of my mind so I said fuck it, there was a bar a half block down, let me go see what's going on their TV maybe they have something other than what I'm watching (reason to get a drink of course) and maybe if I have a drink I'll be able to get my MOJO working again so I headed out. When I got to the bar there were like six people in there. It was a regular spot I would go snagging in so I knew most of the people. But this time there was one slightly older female in there that I hadn't saw before. I mozied around where she was sitting BUT not right next to her because I didn't want to come on too strong.

I sat the third bar stool down to her left. Glancing at the prey on my way to the bar stool I saw she had on a jean skirt. Now on a scale of 1 to 10 she was like a 5, slightly older with some wear and tear and I guessed right, a single mom. She was raising, well raised, her son who was 19 but still living at home. With this skirt on I bump up the ladies on the scale because I love skirts so like the movie said "she had me at hello". I ordered my regular drink double shot Southern Comfort on the rocks and made small talk with the bartender Jim. With Jim there I turned and started to talk to her and asked her "So what brings you here today? I'm kind of a regular, Jim knows that" (now I did this because it's kind of a warm meeting she knows Jim and already talked to him today and I know Jim so I'm a " friend " of his). She said she just needed to get out, she lives with her 19 year old son and she is never home alone…. BINGO that's what I wanted to hear. If there is one thing that will keep a lady coming over to your place is that it's a warm, CLEAN, I mean clean all over and clean smelling place that they will feel comfortable at (AND NOT YOUR MOMS HOUSE OR BASEMENT).

So I sat and let her vent and listened to all the troubles she was having as we were having a few drinks and when ever I refilled I would ask if she needed another. One time she even chuckled and said " No I should be buying your drinks for listening to all my problems like a shrink".

I told her "No I got it, if it weren't for you I'd just be sitting in my apartment by myself and instead I'm sitting here with you having a great conversation with a sexy lady". I asked if she lived close by and she asked the same so I told her

“Yup I live a half block down so when you feel you need a place to go just stop by”. By now I moved to the bar stool right next to her and Jim the bartender was giving me eyes behind her head like “your such a asshole” but come on “she never has alone time” and she came out in a skirt. She was probably so tired of flicking the bean quietly in her shower so her son didn’t hear. She said some day she would love to take me up on it. We continued to drink and B.S.. After she vented for a bit she started laughing and having a good time so since she was feeling better I figured I would slip it in. “Why wait til someday? I got to get going and I can show you where it is right now, plus you got Jim as your witness if you come up missing” and I chuckled. She was feeling good and relaxed from the drinks and being able to vent so she said “Sure I would love to”

SEE this is why you fish in a lake or pond close to your home, apartment, or hotel. When the fish bites and you're reeling it in, the closer you live to the pond the less chance they have to think about what they're doing and talk themselves out of it or come to their senses. We got up to the door and I asked her to come up to see the place.

She was all like “I don’t know if I should”. I said “Come on so you can see I’m a clean person, I don’t want you to think I’m just a messy ass person who cleans when I know I’m going to have guest.”

I opened the door and said “ Want me to go first seeing that you have a skirt on?

" She said " No we're both adults " In my mind I was like Woo Hoo! Like a teen aged kid lol, and we mozied up to the second floor. Man she did have nice tanned legs, some cute sandals and a pink tank top. We get to the top of the stairs and I put my hand in the small of her back and said " Excuse me so I can unlock this door". I opened it up and she was so pleasantly surprised. I gave her the grand tour. One of my bedrooms had a massage table in it and it always peaked the ladies interest. She was like " You must have A LOT of ladies up here" I said " I have a lot of friends up here because they can feel comfortable and relaxed.. She said "Yes I can see how". I asked her if she felt comfortable and she said" Yes and no. I feel comfortable YET I am alone in a strangers apartment". I told her to relax, take a seat and stay a while. I knew she didn't want to be home anyway.

We sat on the couch and I told her to take off her sandals. I asked her when was the last time she got to relax and hang out with a guy alone. She said it was about a year ago. I asked her if she would like a foot massage. I had to throw in the whole " Come on, I'm not a foot fetish guy or anything, I would just like you to be able to relax a little more."

She finally agreed so I put her feet up on my lap and got a little panty shot of her matching pink panties as I was massaging her feet. I knew she knew I had a clear view and she really seemed comfortable with it. With her feet in my lap I got a fucking hard on and I knew she felt it threw my pants on her ankle as I massaged her feet.

I moved my hands from her feet, to her calves, then to her thighs. She didn't stop me. It was as if she were all into it and ready to give me her all. I went in to kiss her, she was panting and breathing as if she had just ran a marathon. She was devouring my tongue like a vampire in heat. I went higher on her thigh up her skirt and was feeling her hot wet pussy through her panties and she finally reached for my cock. She began stroking it through my pants and I told her don't be shy go ahead and take it out. She undid my belt, unzipped my pants and reached in to my boxer briefs. She took my cock out and started to stroke it as if it were water to someone who had been stranded in the desert.

Kissing her and moving down to her neck I pulled my hand up and slowly moved her tank top and bra strap down the side of her shoulder. I cupped her breast with my hand and felt her erect nipple right in the center of my palm. I moved from her neck and started sucking on her erect nipple and flicking her nipple with my tongue. I put my hand back under her skirt and moved her panties to the side to uncover her nice well manicured pussy. She had the Mr. T. cut going on down there.

You know, bald lips all the way through, and a mo hawk above her clit. Her pussy lips were swollen and her pussy was dripping wet. You know some ladies who say they haven't had sex in a while and some how you can tell if they did or they didn't? WELL this one for sure had not. She was quivering with every movement.

I began sliding my two fingers in and out of her pussy as I was sucking on her nipple. When I felt she was wet enough I knelt on the ground right in front of her and with both hands I reached up under her skirt and pulled them pink panties right off leaving her skirt on of course. I don't care how many times you or I have done that before man does it feel great each and every time you pull them panties off a lady! AHHHHHH.

My pants were already unzipped with my cock sticking out and it was throbbing while pointing directly at her. Kneeling between her, I pulled my shirt off and she helped me. I undid her bra and took off her bra and tank top with one swoop. Man did her B cup breasts look so beautiful and perky. I stood up to sit beside her and play with her clit some more but I didn't even get the chance to. She leaned forward just wearing her skirt and it was crumpled up behind her ass so it wasn't covering anything. She reached for my cock as I was standing in front of her and began giving me an extraordinary blow job sucking like a mad woman as she stroked my cock with the other hand.

She took my pants all the way down and reached out and grabbed my thigh for something to hold on to.

I was on cloud 9! To think just a couple hours ago I might of been sitting on this couch alone watching TV. AND did I say ALONE. Well the rest of this story plays along and you may think we fucked like rabbits and she revisited about 5 or 6 times. BUT the point I am trying to make is Ms. Right or Ms. Right Now is out there and needs some cock. So get off your ass and get out there.

CRYSTALIZE

CRYSTALIZE your dreams and goals. I want to use the term goals because dreams are something you want to come true and goals are something that you have a set plan for and you can achieve.

I use the term CRYSTALIZE because you have to see clearly and concisely what you want to achieve, like seeing through a clear crystal. Some people say they want more money, but is that what they really want? Crumbly, dirty, white and green paper? Well true some would look good in stacks on my table, in a briefcase or our hands, but the reality is that MOST people want what the money can bring them in life. A big house, fast car, a lot of beautiful ladies or even freeing up your time. Freeing up time is such a biggie in my book. I always say people get married to spend the rest of their lives together. Yet when we get married we all have to spend at least 40 hours a week away from each other working a daily grind to pay the bills, feed the kids (yea law says I still have to) (KIDDING REALLY) and only take our vacations when allowed. SO one of my crystal clear dreams is to sell enough books, have enough seminars and be able to travel all the time with my wife. I want me being an author to accomplish having all the bills paid, the dream cars, and the nice house.

I'm always learning on a daily basis and constantly feeding my brain new information. So to get down to crystallizing you will need a pen and paper.

You have to write down and be emotional about it when you do, what you are truly thankful for in life. YES I said thankful. If you have nothing to be thankful for you must be a real asshole. Apparently you have other issues that you have to get another book to help you with first. If you're alone go to a mirror and start to picture things and memories in your head. They will come just be creative. We have all had things we can be thankful for, even the little things. Having a job, my kids, being able to dream still. Did you come up with anything yet? Write it down with emotions, and say out loud what you're thankful for EVEN if its just being able to pay your bills this month. You may think you have a very sucky job or a beater of a car and so and so has more than you, BUT that doesn't matter really! Don't concentrate on all that stuff because it takes your mind OFF of all your dreams and goals. If you think you have it bad, think of the MOM and DAD that with the both of them working are not going to be able to pay their mortgage this month. Think of the guy with no arm, or leg. Others have it so much worse in life and achieve so much more. One of the main things you have to do is stay positive and be thankful for all that you do have and achieved up to this point. Appreciate the fact that you still have dreams and desires in life. Enough that you picked up this book or downloaded it.

This is something that you should be thankful for because this means you still have the desire to change your life.

Okay now that you have realized that there are great things you do have in life and you're not focusing on the negative, you can figure out EXACTLY what it is you want in life. Now you have to start writing down what you do want in life. Once again you have to put your creative hat on and bring your emotions out. What do you truly desire in life? Truly? FEEL IT. Where do you want to go? By when do you want to get there? What car do you dream about driving? What color? Can you smell the new interior? I CAN! What bombshell do you want sitting right next to you in that car? See her smile right now! What color hair does she have? What's she wearing? I bet you're looking at her tits right now? That's cool because so am I. Can you feel it? Can you see clearly what you want in life manifesting for you ? Say yes, say YES! Right now from this point forward NO MORE NEGATIVITY OR DOUBTING YOURSELF! One lesson in negativity and this is it, IF you say you can't you're right!!! If you say you can you're also right!! Now put the damn effort into it and get it!

How I work myself is I always set up goals towards what I want. I set up like baby steps sometimes. Maybe it's because I can't multi- task or concentrate.

RIGHT NOW I am COMPLETELY focused and concentrating on this book. I eat, sleep, and breathe this book. I am crystallizing a huge seminar in Costa Rica. where all the men who desire more in life can meet, party and live life to the fullest together.

My outcome of everything is my freedom from my current job that has the golden handcuffs on me. I wanna continue living life to the fullest, spreading the word that anyone can fulfill their dreams and party like a rock star.

Most people in life focus on 90% of what their problems are and 10% of the solution to their problems. DON'T be the everyone else in life. REALIZE the problem with 10% and put 90 % into the solution and move on!

If you are one of the single guys that feels as if you can't talk to ladies, no one wants you or maybe you feel you're a nerd, man get that shit out of your mind. This is another time to reach down grab your pair and get any shadow of a doubt out of your mind that you can't get laid. Crystallize what you want your life to be like. What kind of girls do you want to date? How many a week? It's all out there for the taking and will be there for you once you start taking life by the balls, and get out there and live this wonderful thing called life. Picture how you want to be seen and take baby steps to get there.

Desiring and crystallizing are great but they have to be so much a part of you, in your mind, in your subliminal mind, that you're thinking about what you truly want all the time and what it will bring to you.

Do you have messy greasy hair? Change it! Yellow teeth? Fix that! Nerdy clothing? Well you bought them. Are you slouched down when you walk?

Straighten your ass up and walk with confidence. These are all easy things to change in life, if you don't see change happening and don't take steps to make change happen then fuck it. Put this book down and stay where you are currently at in life.

I once heard a comedian say " Ladies can solve the gas shortage we're facing in this world... if the ladies ONLY fucked the guys who rode the bus". MAN this is so fucking true. Most guys would give up their daily commute in their Porsche and Mercedes once they seen the guys on the bus getting laid. A lot of what guys do in life is to get their little head satisfaction.

SO at this point I need you to start reading and start crystallizing. Crystallize what you truly want in life. Fine tune it to a sharp point like a laser beam, Feel it! Smell it! Taste it! Use all of your imagination and see everything manifesting for you. See it changing your life in front of your eyes.

This is what you have to do EVERY DAY all the time and stay focused. Train your subliminal mind while you're going through everyday life that it is still working towards your goals.

TAKE SOME ACTION

Take some action: I stress this because this is one of the hardest things for our lazy scared asses to do. I say our lazy scared asses because there are many of us that work jobs and we get caught up in the RUTT of life or scared because we think of what other people think of us if we say or do something wrong. These are two main things that keep us where we currently are in life. But really they're excuses and we have to train our subliminal minds right now that we TRULY desire the change in life and this desire has to COMPLETELY conquer the laziness and fears. Sure there are going to be some days we'll want to fall off the face of the earth and relax or days where your game isn't on so you don't feel like talking to that fine ass lady at the gas station and that's cool. You don't have to conquer the world day after day. Just don't have too many of these days because they're so easy to get you stuck right back in the rut of life.

Is there anyone in life that you wonder how they got to where they are in life? Why did they go further in life than you? Or the kicker... Why the hell is she with him? HA HA HA I live that one! Many people wonder why the hell my wife is with me.

The reality was that they had less fear than you and took more action.

If they opened a business, that took action. If they looked up all the information on their business, talked with the proper people and forged onward to open their business, then all of that took action. Could you do this? SURE YOU CAN! If you chose to take some action. I did it from doing a Tony Robbins course. Personal Power II. I opened up an adult book store within four months of doing this course. The course gives you daily exercises to get you off your ass to your goals. It rocks! You have to get it also. Did I know anything about opening an adult book store? NO! But I know working for the average company will not make you rich or bring the retirement everybody dreams of. I didn't have a Tax ID number, a corporation or any companies with the products. I just had a desire for more and pursued it. My desire was big enough that every chance I got I did research, asked questions and pursued my desires. This is the same something that the person you wonder about did. TOOK ACTION!

You really have to get all those excuses and fears out of your life. They will hold you back from a lot of experiences in life, and there are a shit load of fucking awesome experiences that you don't want to miss. Believe me. I don't care how old you think you are or how ugly you think you are, or how broke you think you are.

You can live out all of your dreams and goals as long as you honestly and truly take some action on a daily basis to get there.

Back to the guy you seen or know, thinking how and why the hell is she with him? UHH because he had the balls to talk to her. He had some confidence in his nut sack and probably made her laugh. As a matter of fact you should take notes on what the fuck he does where ever you see him. How he dresses, how he interacts with people, etc. because apparently something is working for him. Don t hate, learn and duplicate.

If you haven't noticed by now I kind of have two tracks I'm writing in this book that I jump back and forth to. One track is kind of a no matter what you want in life you can have tips and strategies guide to help you try and achieve them and track two is building confidence and tips for guys to go out in life and get the girl and hopefully some pussy.

I always went for the underdogs in life.. and I always try and help everybody prevail. One of my action steps on a grand scale is to reach out there and change lives in men who desire more. I always have parties and hopefully someday I will have all you men who I have helped spark in life, change, or inspire to do more at one of my huge parties or I will be invited to yours.

My action plan that I have is to spew a plethora of life experiences I have been through all over these pages in attempts to complete a book.

Then I want to get out there meet everybody at seminars and parties and hear all of your success stories of your businesses, life successes, and your crazy ass stories of how you got laid and see your hot ass ladies.

I have a huge task on my hands and I'm taking action right now, not playing 360, or gambling at the casinos, or sitting in front of the TV (where everyone on the TV is getting paid but you're not getting paid for watching it).

Now back to you taking some action. Even a little bit of action like 10% per day. Just 10 % per day. Would that be too much of a commitment if it can change your life? Do one thing a day towards achieving your goals, you can chose how much effort per day, and what you do per day will determine how fast you wanna change your life. I've studied three courses where three different guys made almost a million dollars in about sixteen months time. So it is completely possible. NO EXCUSES from this day forward from YOU OR ME. You have the desire, you have the dream crystallized, now what do you have to do to get there?

If you want to start a business you need a business plan. The fastest way is to just Google business plans and BAM there are free templates.

There are also companies that will do them for you. You wanna get some dates and pussy? Start communicating with all the ladies you see.

When I say communicate remember that even a smile and a polite friendly hello count as communicating. If you don't know what you wanna take action on, well now is a good time to decide. If you want more money what are you gonna do to get it? Write a book or open up an online business maybe? Do you have a hobby you wanna turn into your career? How about a hot dog cart? Don't laugh they are great money making opportunities. Are you already a business person? What will it take to get you to the next level? No bullshit. Right now you probably already know what it is that will make you more money or take you to the next level. So why aren't you doing it and why aren't you there?

If you wanna get that fine piece of new suki suki ass, why aren't you talking to her? Did you take your ass out to the store yet? Did you get some great smelling cologne yet? I'm not talking High Karate or soap on a rope either. While you're there pick up some crest 3-D white toothpaste (white teeth make a huge difference). Smile, laugh and talk with every lady you have a chance to make small talk with. Wanna lose some weight? You have to extremely desire it all the time. How will it change your life if you lose all the weight you wanna lose right now? What is the true reason you wanna lose the weight?

Figure that out and make it a burning desire and take some action. Start with going for a thirty minute walk after a small meal instead of watching TV. There are plenty of ladies out walking or at the gym to talk to. SEX is a good reason to lose weight, it will give you a strong desire. But also let me stress that it's not necessary.

There are a lot of ladies out there who like big guys also. If you lack confidence because you think you can't get a lady because you're a big guy take some action for that and get out there. Go out and look around for the guys your size or bigger with female partners and you'll see that's all in your mind.

The life you're looking for **IS** there for you!! Ask the universe for it!! Desire it!! Believe you can achieve it!! Go for it!! Achieve it!! We are all here for you and here to support you. I cant wait till we meet and hear your stories.

OK here is some erotica for your ass to get that desire going. But you have to promise me something. When you finish this chapter you have to get your ass up and take some sort of action. I want you to succeed and get all you desire in life, party like a rock star and hear all of your stories.

The Kwik Kwikie: I always host a lot of parties and I have my friends invite friends. I tell all the guys we have to provide all the drinks for the ladies. A good party is a party with a lot of ladies but a great party is a party with a lot of beautiful tipsy ladies.

I always tell all the guys at the parties " work the room" talk to everyone at the party, small talk and don't be a stalker! SO this party was at my bachelor pad, YES I did use that retro 70's term bachelor pad, a second floor apartment above a vacant business.

It was a two bedroom apartment with the bedroom in the front a total Sodom and Gomorrah room complete with massage table, paddles, whips, dildos, vibes, and massagers all on display to be seen. Of course there was a shit load of anti bacterial hand soap, baby wipes, clean sheets and towels as well. This bedroom was right off the front room where I had some candles and club lights set up as a dance floor. Down the hall was the bathroom, then the kitchen and my bedroom was the back bedroom right off of the kitchen. Well in this little two bedroom apartment at this particular party we had about forty people. A lot of my friends were couples because I would normally " MASSAGE" the wife while the hubby watched or joined in to help me "MASSAGE" his wife. The couples and guys would normally bring single ladies because come on, who doesn't like a good freaky party. The couple that brought this particular lady who caught my eye that night brought her because she was their play toy and they wanted me to "massage" as they watched and played together. During the party I couldn't read her vibe at all. My friend's wife was dancing with me and grabbing my cock as he sat on the couch watching with their play toy sitting next to him. The front room lights were off.

The only lights lighting the room were the candles and the multicolored club light dancing around to the beat of the music. There were about twelve couples dancing all crowded in this little space. We were all feeling good and drinking. The room was hot and the ladies looked great with the sweat glistening off of their skin.

I was working the whole party like I normally do but their play toy they brought was being quiet, I mean it was like pulling teeth talking to her. I was thinking man she wasn't feeling me and that was cool because there were a lot of options at the party. I saw that one of my buddies was talking to a lady and they mozied off into the “massage” room together. When little MS. Personality saw this she left into the kitchen. I was like wow maybe they didn't debrief her on how we partied before they came. I stood dancing with two other hotties on the make shift dance floor and the couple who brought her followed her to the kitchen. Man if its one thing I like it's hot girls having FUN and dirty dancing. I felt like Patrick Swayze -“I'm having the time of my life”. As I'm getting jiggy with it I see my lovely friend with her play toy coming back from the kitchen with some mixed drinks in hand heading right to the dance floor. I guess they followed her to the kitchen to pull the stick out of her ass. Finally she was letting loose and getting crazy on the dance floor. My lady friend who brought her was all over her feeling her up and they were going at it right on the dance floor.

It was like I was watching a porno, man they were dancing crazy and I was salivating watching. At this moment I realized how fucking tall she was. OMG she had to be like 5'9” to 5”11” but she did have some big ass titties and they were looking prime as she was dancing and they were getting all felt up on. I figured here it goes I was going to try and dance with her and maybe get a face full of breast. Yep them lumps them lovely lady lumps.

While we were dancing all the ladies surrounded me and it was like I was surrounded by a plethora of boobies. I was loving life to the fullest. I finally had a chance to ,make my move. I pulled my friends hubby to the dance floor to dance with her, the two hot blonds went to refill their drinks and I got my alone time with who I will now call Heather. She began to small talk over the music and she danced very good. I dance all the time, you know that saying dance like nobody is watching? Yes that's me, dancing like nobody is watching and doing my version of the two step slash rusty out dated intoxicated robot lol. For being a slightly bigger girl she was wearing some tight jeans and man were they looking great.

About 2 am she had to go. I was like damn we didn't even have time to play. But maybe I could set something up for another day. My couple friend asked if I could walk her to the door, they were still dancing and hooked up with another couple. So I was like cool it gives me a chance to talk to her one on one.

She actually grabbed my hand and headed to the door then walked down the stairs. I was behind her feeling good while looking at her long hair and fine ass booty in them tight jeans. As we got to the final step and before she opened the final door I realized that if she walks out this chance may be gone forever. So yes I reached down grabbed my pair and spoke the fuck up and asked for her number so we can possibly hook up some other day. But she had another agenda, she leaned down towards me and started kissing me hot and heavy.

MAN I was so down with that, we were standing there at the bottom of the stairs making out as I had a full apartment of people upstairs. We were tonguing hot and heavy and feeling each other up and my cock was already hard from walking behind her down the stairs while I was thinking of all the dirty things I wanted to do to her. She was stroking my cock through my pants and I was trying to undo her Fort Knox bra trying to get them huge fucking jugs out so I can suck on them pancake sized nipples. But as soon as one boob popped out the bra she already went down and had my cock in her mouth. Mind you this is about 2 am, we are in my hallway and I still have a house full of people with a party going on upstairs. She was grabbing my balls tightly as she was sucking and deep throating my cock making all the same sounds as a porn star. As she was sucking away I had one hand holding her hair up so I could see her nice juicy lips wrapped around my cock. I had my other hand trying to undo her jeans.

I finally got them undone and half way down enough to feel her hot wet juicy pussy. I am playing with her clit and dying to taste her pussy because it drove me crazy in them jeans all night. I moved back, got my cock out of her mouth and leaned her back against the wall and went down to indulge in her sweet juices. Man this pussy was nice, shaved and completely swollen with ecstasy. I was lapping it up like a thirsty dog and she was grabbing my head holding me as close to her as possible. We were getting just the right pressure because I could feel the juices gushing and hear the moans of her pleasure.

I tried taking her pants all the way off but she was like "No someone might come down." So I stood there licking her pussy as best I could with her pants just below her knees as I fingered her. My cock was throbbing so bad and her pussy was dripping wet so I got up and put my cock in her willing pussy as she leaned with her back up against the wall. I was like just hitting it with the tip. DAMN this never happened before,, ha ha ha she was too fucking tall. I was hard and ready to fuck and not going to let this stop me because I knew she was ready for some cock. I bent her over, stepped up onto the first step and inserted my throbbing cock and started pounding away. She was primed and ready to pop with all the foreplay but I was like YEA I was feeling great. I had a nice ass bent over right in front of me so I was going to drive this home. I was grabbing her waist and ass gripping and holding on as I pounded away.

I finally had to pop myself and I knew I had a load of cum to shoot from all my excitement but there was no where to blow my load at and I didn't know if she was feeling it on her boobs or down the chute. I pulled it out and she stood up and grabbed it as if she knew that I was so ready to cum and she stroked my cock and pointed it right down the hallway and BAAM like a howitzer cannon three huge streams shot all the way down the hallway.. then the after shocks were shooting out. We both were on cloud 9 still moaning, laughing and having a blast. She started pulling her pants up and saying "I really have to go." I was like "You sure you don't want to come back up stairs?" and she said " **No I am so late. I have to pick up my boyfriend"..... WHOMP WHOMP WHOMP.**

I just wasted a minute of your life

Time is an extreme luxury in life that you can NEVER get back. Every second, minute, hour and day that passes is gone forever.

Not only is it the time that passes, it's also your youth. I am sure there are guys from 18 to at least 65 reading this book. For some I hope this may build their confidence and they will be early bloomers and party their whole life. I hope that I can help the late bloomers realize that life is still out there and you can change how you're living it this instant. When you finish this chapter I hope you realize the importance of you being happy and living the life you always dreamed of. Currently I am 40 and still partying like a rock star. I've had a good solid 22 years of living how I wanted and seizing the day plenty of times. I'm not saying this to brag, I'm just saying I really am kind of an average Joe like most of the men reading this book. I just chose to live life to the fullest.

Okay let's talk ages and why you shouldn't let time pass you by. If you're a young buck you still got plenty of time so just grab that pair and start talking, break down those walls of your comfort zone and don't look back. If you're an older gentlemen who wants to change, don't ever think you're too old.

Look at Sylvester Stallone, at the time of this book he is 65 years old and still living life to the fullest. Jack Nicholson is 74. Man 74 years old and still living life like a rock star! How many years does he have on you? Really think about it. That's that many years you have to do what ever it is you want. Start living today! Okay, lets keep going- Francois Henri Pinault you may not have ever even known who this guy is, but he is 75 years old and banging Salma Hayek. This lucky son of a so and so is a billionaire and married to her. Now if he is 75 and still pulling Honeys like Salma, what the heck are you waiting for??? Okay okay, I have one more, Hugh Hefner, the stud of all studs is 85 years old. Compare his age to yours. Me personally, I'm 40 and that's 45 more years I have to go. That's double the years I've been alive, so why spend that time NOT being happy? How many fine, beautiful chins do you think them wrinkly, saggy balls came across?

I know, I know, you're probably thinking their rich and famous. I'm not even talking about money right now, I'm talking about living life. Yes money helps getting ass and we all should choose to conquer the world and make more money, but I'm just trying to put into prospective that you're never too old to do what you want to do in life or make a change. Many people flow like a river and take "the path of least resistance" and flow around the rocks in life...Fuck that!! I always say if someone is willing to stop my progress, fuck em!
I say what I wanna say and keep on keeping on while making more money.

Why let one asshole who may have crossed paths with you, piss you off or something? Why waste any more minutes thinking about that person than you have to? There is way better and more productive things to have on your mind than that asshole. Like for instance, how about that beautiful lady you saw earlier today or yesterday? What was she wearing? Was it sexy? How was her hair? Did you get a whiff of her scent? Did you get a good look at her ass, tits or camel toe? Did you talk to her? Run that back in your mind... How would your dream meeting with her have been? Would you have pulled up in a Porsche or a Mercedes? Were you dressed all dap? What cologne did you have on? You already caught her eye and scent, did you speak to her? Did you make her laugh?

See, now isn't that better to have on your mind instead of some jerk in life? Fuck em! Make more money, get more girls, party harder and don't look back.

I hope when you have finished the last chapter you took some action whether it be looking up business info, going for a run or doing push ups, or talking to a fine filly. The point to me writing all this is for you to become more confident and take some action in life. Make a change...

So I'm ending this chapter right now. I need you to start taking some deep breaths, put your shoulders back and be extremely confident right now. Just you and me. Get pumped up and tell me what you want in life.

Now put some headphones on and turn up a fucking kick ass song that motivates you and go have a kick ass day! Seize the day and be more confident and talk to people! Grab them balls brada!

FUCK THE WORLD BE HAPPY

Okay there are many people in this world that don't succeed because they worry what other people think. They worry way too much what other people think. When I say succeed I am talking about at business, sports, and pulling honeys. We are a creature of conforming to society not making waves, and followers of a plain group of people that don't even know where the heck they are going. STOP, STAND UP and look around you. Is that really where you want to go? Apparently not if you're here reading this book. I always say " I wanna go to hell because that's where the bad girls are". But maybe I am already there because there are bad girls all around us. Me and you! You just have to take off them plain, rose colored, conform with society glasses and notice them. They're all around.

Whats one thing you want to do right now but don't because your afraid of what people might think of you? First of all fuck them!! and tell me. What are you afraid of? Failure? Being ridiculed? Hell I take my hat off to all who are around me who are trying something new. **If you never try anything new you will never know what may be.** You'll stay where you currently are in life right now and apparently that isn't where you want to be. Now if you're content with where you're at, that's cool also as long as that's TRULY where you want to be.

Not because you're conforming or you're there because someone else wants you there. Apparently there is some part of you in your mind that wants more. Why did you buy this book? REALLY? Are you bottling up your dreams? Keeping them all safe and secure inside of you so they won't be ridiculed? Man I've been there and done that, sowed enough oats for at least fifty to one hundred men, but you have to figure out what you want in life and what's more important to you. I almost lost everything in life out there being a knuckle head because I didn't follow my own chapter two in this book. This was because I wasn't being completely honest with my special someone and thinking with my other head. So I share with you, fuck the world and be happy, but keep those close to your heart and your mind in consideration while you're moving on.

At some point you're going to have to find a balance in life. On one spectrum you want to conquer the world but you have to maintain the happiness in your family life... and this is for the married men. You single guys... I'll meet you in Costa Rica at one of my seminars and you all can party with me and my wife all week long. But the married ones be careful. **Married or single men, If it's business then KICK ASS and take names don't be shy, don't be afraid to speak up. Ask questions and get what you want out of life.** When it comes to ladies the funny thing is I bet your wife or significant other can bring home more fine ass ladies then you.

You know another funny thing that makes me laugh? When some guy oogles at younger ladies and someone says "She is young enough to be your daughter" The reality is that most porn companies contract these fine ass sexy willing ladies on their 18th birthday. Its usually the guy ridiculing you the loudest that is in the viewing booth at a adult book store watching a porno beating off to her. Fuck the world be happy, as long as you are not harming anybody, invading anyone else's space, or being obnoxious (I really dislike obnoxious people) HAVE AT IT! Have fun! Do what you want to do in life! Live life to the fullest!

Don't be afraid of what people think if you fail... Fuck them, Don't ever have that on your mind. **Why think about failure when you can be dreaming of success,** and when you do get there I want a special invite to your party.

Happiness is contagious and so easy to spread. People love being happy and in a happy environment. Happy fun people get invited out and get invited to parties. So stop being Mr. Negative Ass Party Pooper. Brush that shit off, don't sweat the small stuff, and get your ass back in to the game of life. It's like when you were younger, skins vs the shirts were the happy go lucky people out enjoying life and were competing against the doubting ass negative doubting Thomas stick in the mud... What side is it that you want to be on again?

Well I'm team captain and I'm choosing you right now to be on my side and you better be willing to step up to the plate and party your ass off at my next party. Start that business you always wanted,

I know that you can bring the heat, get up off that damn bench the other team has you on and bring your ass to my side where you will start living your life to the fullest today!

Our team will be here to help you succeed and make them changes in life with all the moral support necessary and where you'll be taught how to get that oral support you crave. HA HA HA that was funny right?

So since you started reading this book have you started making those changes that I have been preaching to you? Did you buy some new cologne? Some good shit! Have you asked any co worker ladies what they like? Now don't go saturating yourself in it when you go out just a hint fucker. Have you gotten yourself invited to any parties? DID YOU GO? And did you bring something? A bottle of booze? A six pack? Some flowers for the lady of the house? Or a kick ass gift? And the biggie... Did you work the room?

I really hope by now that you are making some changes and are planning on us meeting up someday. Like you inviting me to your grand opening, the first party you host, the multi million

dollar home you sold party, or your first book signing party.

I really want you to break down those walls of your comfort zone, man just see yourself doing it in your creative mind and it will emanate into your life. Reach down grab your pair and start living! YOU'RE ON MY TEAM NOW!

THE FUCK FEST

You can skip this chapter if you would like, this chapter is not a motivational chapter or a self improvement chapter. It's a story about a fuck fest that I went to.

This chapter is just to let you know that this shit is real and there are parties out there where beautiful ladies, alcohol and pussy are a plenty. I stumbled upon this party through a editorial in a mid west monthly publication called " The Gentlemen s Pages". It's free to pick up at any adult book store around the Chicago land area or you can Google search for it and subscribe. This is a free plug for them. They used to be ran out by a distributor for my adult book store whom I bought product from.

Anyway the writer of this editorial wrote about the honest and truly group gang bangs going on around the Chicago land area. Not only did the writer write about the fuck fest, if you read into the article he also wrote how to find these parties and get invited to them.

Some being my perverted self read in depth on how to find and access this live version of Sodom and Gomorrah. I started to search the web like a Basset hound searching for his masters freshly shot duck.

I joined some free local groups on yahoo and voila with in about a week I got my first invite threw my email for such a mythical party. There was a format and protocol to follow there was a number to call and I had to RSVP. I was told if I did RSVP and not show I wouldn't be allowed to any other party that she (the hostess) was throwing. At this party I was told that she was hosting for four ladies who dreamed of being gang banged and they desired as many cocks as can be mustered up for their special event. I was told that you must be clean, and have protection. I was hoping when she said protection that she didn't mean a bullet proof vest because it would be in a bad area. To my surprise it was being held in a suite at a prominent hotel in the O'hare International area.

There would be a fee for attending but I already knew about this from the article. It wasn't a fee to pay a pimp, the hostess reserves a three bedroom suite with kitchen. She then tallied the cost of the suite and split that with the guys attending and this was fair to me. The attendance fee came out to be about twenty bucks and there was about twenty five guys who showed.

I was instructed to meet up at a well known sports bar in the O'hare area and look for a table with a yellow balloon tied to a birthday bag. Believe it or not Murphys law struck my ass this night. I got a damn flat tire heading up there on the expressway about 8:30 at night.

I was mother fucking the whole time I was changing the flat tire. I knew I had to be there by 9:00 pm so I changed my flat as fast as a NASCAR pit crew. I still had to stop at the store for some condoms and booze. I got the tire changed, shot right to a 7/11, picked up some go go juice (My Southern Comfort) and asked the guy behind the counter for 5 boxes of condoms. You should of seen the guy's and lady's face behind the counter. I said "Yea I got a party I am heading to and yes its like that." The guy asked if he could go with me. Little did I know that in the future that I would be writing about it and inviting all who read my books to party with me.

I finally got to the bar with about fifteen minutes to spare and found the yellow balloon tied to the birthday bag and a fully packed back of the bar. I didn't know who was with the party so I went to the nice looking red head sitting with the balloon. She actually had a log of all the screen names that RSVP'd. She greeted me with a big hug and told me it was nice to meet me, asked what I RSVP'd under, marked my name off and told me to go mingle. She pointed out five other ladies that were planning to live out their fantasies and told me to go say hi.

First things first, I headed to the bathroom because I was covered in sweat from changing that tire and my hands were all dirty so I went to wash up. When I got back to the bar I grabbed a shot to relax.

There were two guys sitting at the bar that apparently read the same article and went on the same treasure hunt as I. We started to talk and bullshit and hung together like high school buddies that met in orientation.

Within ten minutes the hostess's boyfriend inconspicuously approached all the guys with a clip board that contained the guest list and the hotel room receipt with all the math done out. Our split would be twenty-five bucks. Cool. We put our share in and got a little make shift map to the hotel with the suite number on it. The hotel was about five minutes from the bar. Within five minutes of all the guys receiving their map there was a mass exodus from the bar.

We all pulled into the parking lot and there was a guy at the side door letting people in and telling them to be quiet and go right up to the room. The hallways were so quiet you could have heard a rat fart. We all walked up the stairs to the suite. Walking into the suite was a gorgeous site. You walked into a living room with a circular fire place in the center of the room, with a big TV. To the left there was a full kitchen and small dining area where the hostess was fixing snacks on the counter top. To one side of the front room there was one bedroom and on the complete opposite side there was two bedrooms with a bathroom in the middle.

I put my party bag in the dining room , grabbed my Southern Comfort out of it and started to mingle around the place.

First I went to the kitchen where the hostess was being swarmed by guys trying to flirt with her and telling her how beautiful and sexy she was. Then I went to the single bedroom where a forty-ish blonde was already naked sitting on the edge of the bed being eaten out while she was sucking another mans cock.

I was like WOW good shit Maynard. I mozied to the front room where a interracial couple was sitting down warming up or maybe she had cold feet. I decided to sit there with them and B.S. for a while because I am a good bullshitter and I can bring out the freak in most people. (Hello hence me writing this book) I sat down and found out quite a bit about them, I actually got their number to hook up with them at a later date. After a little conversation I excused myself and made it to the other two rooms.

In the room to the right there was a sexy thick black lady with huge tits as big as my head butt naked bent over the bed with a big brada fucking the hell out of her. Man this guy could have been like a porno pro with his huge cock and she seemed as if she were really enjoying it. There was already five other naked guys in line right behind him watching and enjoying the show as they stroked their cocks to keep them hard.

By now I'm half pint in and feeling real good so I unbuttoned my button down shirt and made it to the last room where I find the red headed hostess laying at the end of the bed on her back.

A guy with a T-shirt on and nothing else was holding her legs on his shoulders and beating that shit up like she was Rodney King. There was about ten guys in her room watching and apparently she was well known for being the most outgoing. As she was lying on her back she looked and saw me standing in the door way and motioned to me to come closer.

I was feeling so good by now that I walked right up to her and she told me right off the bat "Stick your cock in my mouth." WOW that was a ice breaker for me. So there I was pants and boxer briefs off and just a button down shirt on straddling her mouth as she was laying down pumping my cock into her mouth doing push ups over her. The guy was still beating it up while I was in her mouth and she was in sheer ecstasy. I was fucking her mouth as if I were fucking her from behind. The more I fucked her mouth and shoved it in the more she enjoyed it. By this time the guy who was fucking her blew his load and she motioned me to get up and she laid me on my back. She bent over the bed and started giving me a bodacious blow job and another guy jumped right in behind her.

While she was sucking my cock I looked over to the side and a guy was motioning me to see if I would switch up with him. So when I moved to the side she started to suck his cock but kept a firm grip on mine stroking it.

At this time the guys at the party were all warming up, coming closer and enjoying the festivities. I finally got her tiger clinch released and mozied to the other room where the forty-ish blonde that was being eaten while sucking cock was making a a lot of noise but really not fucking. She was butt naked riding a guy but barely moving.

So I went to the room where the twenty-five year old sexy thick black chick was fucking like a champ and to my surprise the other lady with cold feet that was sitting on the couch was sitting at the end of the bed with her dress up and her thong to the side with a guy fingering her... well three fingering her.

It seemed like there is where the party was going to end up being so I went to my party bag and got my baby wipes out and cleaned up. I grabbed some condoms and went back to the room. By the time I got back there the the red headed hostess was in there also 69ing the twenty-five year old and they were both being fucked at the same time. The shy lady was in the middle of both of them sucking on their nipples kinda doggy style trying to squeeze in. I saw she was willing to play so I stood up on the bed and went to her side and was fingering her from behind and had my other hand on her upper back.

I motioned to her with a condom in my hand to see if it was okay and she gave me this very cute smile and nodded go ahead.

I put the condom on and so couldn't believe I was fucking this hot lady. In public guys would probably be shy to talk to her, but here she was at a gang bang in all her glory.

I was standing up in the middle of the bed fucking her doggy style and like a T she was licking the nipples of the ladies laying across the bed 69ing and there was a guy on each side of the bed fucking those ladies.. now come on guys this is some hardcore raunchy porno shit. Never in my wildest dreams did I think that the party would be going as good as it had been.

By now the room was jam packed because this is where the party was. The red headed hostess says "Okay guys I need some cum" she got off the bed and moved into the center of the room where she knelt down. She again said "Guys I want cum all over my face". So I got off the bed and took my condom off and about four other guys circled her, it was like gambling fun, pop after pop all five of us completely covered her face with cum.

It was dripping all over her tits, she was moaning all crazy and was rubbing it all over her. She was like having an organism as she was being bathed in cum. After I shot my load I got up and went back to my play bag to freshen up.

On my way back I noticed yet another blonde who showed up in the bedroom right off the kitchen. She was in there sucking cock already.

At this time it was already about 3am and I was toast. I still had to make it all the way back to the south side so I left. This was just one experience of my many and if this is what you're looking for believe me it's sure out there for you.

Life's too short to be stuck where you currently are right now.

You can have anything you want as long as your desire is always there and you're always striving for it. Maybe on this day this wild and crazy party is what I desired, it had to be some part of my interest or on this night I wouldn't of made it there. Where do you think some strange growth may take you? How does the song go "life is a Highway and I want to ride it all night long".

God speed my friend there are many experiences in life that you nor I have experienced yet, but I'm hope I'm giving you as much desire as I still have to experience everything in life that's out there.

My law of numbers

Numbers numbers numbers! Life really is a numbers game to me. Whatever you wanted to accomplish, host, or sell it's all about the numbers. It goes for selling real estate, getting a job, or getting laid. You have to get out there, interact with enough people, make contacts and leave a good impression. The more times you make contact the more chances you have of getting what you want.

Want to make $1 million in real estate? Talk to fifty people a day. Fifty quality people a day. Want to make $1 million selling books? Sell 100,000 copies of one book or sell 100,000 copies of ten different books that you wrote. Want to get laid once a week? Go out and talk to thirty ladies a week. The great thing about you being laid is that you can make them feel comfortable and these become quality contacts for repeat visits. Your success at whatever you do comes from numbers.

Get a calculator and figure out how some numbers you need will work for you in what ever you want to accomplish.
Start figuring out what you need to succeed. You must know that everything you do isn't going to be a home run or a success story and that's why you need to plan on putting up some big numbers. Whatever doesn't work is not a failure if you learn from it.

You have to realize that you're a failure if you don't keep trying but if you keep trying and it still doesn't work out just keep learning and change your approach like Thomas Edison. If he would've quit after ten tries we would not have the light bulb, if he would've quit after one hundred tries we would not have the light bulb. No matter how many times his light bulb did not work he kept on trying and kept on changing his approach therefore we now have the light bulb. This is one gentleman who kept playing the numbers game. He put away the naysayers by not listening to them and created what he wanted to create. He followed his desires and dreams just like I'm asking you to do.

This is the first book I am writing and publishing and if I only sell ten copies, guess what, I learned how to get a book published, edited and created. It will be that much easier for me to do my next time around. If I write ten books and only ten people a month buy one of each book that's one hundred books a month in sales. See it goes back to Rob's law of numbers.

So what's your hustle going to be? How are the law of numbers going to work for you?

Go ahead tell me. Explain it to me. Go look in the mirror and pretend it's me on the other side and sell me on your numbers game. What do you have to do to change your sales game? To change your hustle or change your life?

If I were to tell you that in six months we're heading to Costa Rica again and you can party with some of the most beautiful ladies in the world and that the hotel the expenses and airfare will be about $1500 what would you have to do to make it there to party with us? Breaking it down that's $250 per month you would have to put away. That's $125 per payday or $125 every two weeks you would have to come up with. It is just a numbers game but to win in it you have to give yourself goals and deadlines to make with the numbers. This relates to all you want to do in life. Put away money for a family vacation, put away money for a down payment on a house, make an extra hundred thousand dollars per year or maybe an extra million dollars per year.

Look up Brendon Buchard in Google. He can show you how he made an extra $4.8 million dollars in eighteen months. He had the desire for change. Not only to change his life but to help change other peoples lives. It may be hard to believe but it comes down to your own desire to make that change in your life. Your commitment to yourself . When you see someone you want to approach or talk to don't let them steal your thunder. They may be the one that holds the key to your million dollar sale, or hold the Holy Grail of the party that you'll meet Ms. Right. Talk to everyone no matter what you are looking for. When you talk to everybody don't think of it as just trying to sell them something, just be yourself happy-go-lucky and fun loving.

Start with baby steps by just talking to them or by just saying hi. You'll know when you're ready because you'll feel your confidence level step up. You start making conversations from there. Remember if you feel you messed up in this conversation or the next one it's not a failure. Put that behind you because there's billions of people in this world to keep talking to. If you're in business or selling something pass your business card on, if you're looking to take somebody out to dinner, give or get a phone number. It is a lot easier now with the text messaging and Facebook. People more easily give you their Facebook information or phone number to text.

Life is a big numbers game. The more numbers you put up the more people you talk to the more information you feed your brain the better chances of getting what you want in life. Another numbers game you should teach yourself to play is to be a reader or a student of success. A student of what you want to do or become in life. Everything you want to become or do has a written book, an audio book or old-school hardcover book for you to learn from. I always feel the best way to do a book is in your car on CD or download it to your phone or iPod and listen in your car on your daily grind to and from work since you're sitting for thirty minutes to an hour every day. Why not teach yourself something when you're sitting there.

There are books on sales, marketing, self-improvement, dating, whatever you're looking for there is a plethora of books out there to download and become a master at.

Don't forget none are a waste of time if you learn at least one thing from it. Don't be a doubting Thomas saying “Oh that wasn't worth my money.” There is at least one thing you heard or you read in that book that you could of learned and if you didn't listen to it again or read it again.

Become a master of who you want to be. Want to be a real rock star? Take real guitar lessons! Want to be like Donald Trump? First of all buy all his books and all his courses and study him to the T to find out where his mindset is. Then follow what he says to do to purchase the real estate! What do you really honestly and truly desire in life? You tell me. Let's put together a plan and sell it to you and your subliminal mind. Go for it! Right now sit down and put a numbers goal in your head of a minimal number of people you can talk to about anything. Not the same lady you see at the store every day. Fucker don't try and become a slick Willie, you'll only be cheating yourself. Really get out there and meet new people every day. Get gas from a different gas station, buy your lottery tickets from a different store. When you're going to the store to buy something stand in the longest line where you see a female not the shortest line just to get out of the store. There now you have a captive audience try talking to her. Make small talk.

Be exotic and creative when you're playing the numbers game. Like a particular ethnicity? Go to area were there's a majority of that ethnicity.

There was a fifty something year old guy who knew I had a massage place opened and he noticed the bulge I used to have in my pants, no not my cock, my knot of money I used to walk around with. He came up to me one day and asked if I had the time to sit down with him and talk business. I really wasn't looking for a business partner at this time, but I'm always looking to help anybody or answer questions if I can. Maybe he wanted to make a change in his life. He knows I'm always talking about success and positive people and positive speaking so maybe this is why I was thinking he wanted to talk business. He offered to take me to dinner so we set up a date and I went. He was a fifty something year old in debt and wanted a way out. He knew all about my past businesses and asked if there were any way that I would be able to manage him and if there will be a market for him. You know it's hard for a guy to break into the massage business since there are so many guys out there that will massage a lady for free. But there are a lot of niche markets and he may fit into one of them. This was a very distinguished gentleman for fifty years old. He still had a nice toned body, great conversation skills and he told me he had a ten inch cock so I figured he had a great shot because there was a great deal of guys that would love to see their ladies with the guy with the cock of this size.

Don't think of me as crazy! There are a lot of couples out there that love boy toys and there are a lot a guys that want to visually see their significant others perform like a porn star with a guy similar to porn star size.

I told him I was interested in managing him but I would attempt to help him break into the industry. I had him get a gym membership, shave his beard, and "just for men" his hair. I filled him in on my law of numbers and where to advertise at. I even reviewed his pictures that he put in his ads, No I didn't meet gaze fucker. I just wanted to help this guy succeed like I help anybody succeed. He started out a little slow going on appointments. The funny thing is he didn't even need a massage table. He lived the more upscale life as it was so those were more his clientele. They would take him out to dinner, take him to concerts, and put him up in hotel rooms. Man he was living the life that most guys would want to and he was fifty years old. He just had to remember to keep it discreet and don't blab his mouth about the couples he was with. We still keep in touch. Last I talked to the gentleman in twelve months he made $103,000! Isn't that fucking nuts? A guy that thought nobody would be attracted to him with nowhere else to turn because he was in debt is now living his life like most men dream.

Sometimes your fear is what gets you moving! When your mortgage is due and you have a fear of losing your house doesn't it become more motivating to you to get off your ass and do something?

Normally fear is what keeps you from moving ahead in life, but in this instance it is fear that got him moving forward in life. Another story of a introvert into extrovert living life to the fullest and partying like a rock star. Don't you think it's your turn!?!

Shape up, smell good, get some!

This chapter is kind of self-explanatory, the title of it says it all. In layman's terms don't be a wrinkly sweaty stink bomb. Contrary to your beliefs your clients and or the ladies that you're interested in notice things such as personal hygiene. But don't worry hygiene and clothes are easy to change and can be fun if you use this as a tool **(and** not be a tool).

Hygiene is a must. Guys go ahead and do a self-evaluation right now. Goldfish to you in the mirror, are the standard yellow? You still have coffee breath from this morning? Its 7pm damn it! Why do you still have coffee breath? You may not notice but guess what everyone around you does. This is very easy to fix (unless you need dental work) but at least clean the teeth you do have. The easiest thing to start with is that damn breath. If you're out reading this right now pick up some gum or some breath strips. Stay away from them clickity clack tic-tacs they make too much noise in your pocket when you walk. While you're out pick up some crest 3-D white. I really love crest 3-D white and I swear by it. You should be brushing your teeth three times a day, but if for some reason you can't swing that at least do it twice in the morning and right before you go to bed.

Many of you are probably like "who doesn't know this" well there are guys out there that really don't and I'm talking to them being the friend they need and helping them out. Just like if I'm out and someone is talking to me with a booger hanging out of their nose, I'm the type of person who tells them. I would rather have them take care of it right now then go through the rest of the day with a booger hanging out of their nose. So brush them fangs and if you look in the mirror and they are still really bad and if you got the money go get them taken care of. Guys put yourself in that females shoes. Would you kiss a female if her mouth smelled like ass and her teeth looked like crap? Well touche you don't want that to be what she sees our smells.

While you're there in the mirror, do you see little military men repelling from the nose hairs shooting out your nose? Man that annoys me so much when talking to someone with them ape hangers coming out their nose I just want to pull them out myself. I'm talking about your nose hairs guys, you need to trim them damn things because when you're talking with people seriously and all they can concentrate on is your nose hairs peeking out your nose there is a problem.

Is your face greezy? I didn't say greasy I said greezy. Oh my god there is a huge difference, there is a lot of different facial products out there so if you feel you need some just buy some. You know it all comes down to basic hygiene.

How about your butta? (that's your hair) You know I'm not here to keep busting your chops or to make anybody a cookie-cutter boyfriend. Keep yourself clean and smelling good. If you have the grunge look, make sure is the grunge look. There is a difference between the grunge look and looking like major bed head. If you have long hair take care of your long hair, wash it and condition it, and no matter how you wear it just make sure the look isn't greasy. Some ladies love long hair and some ladies love bald heads. You can't make that choice nor could I that's just their personal choice.

As for your beard or mustache that's your complete personal choice whatever it is just try to keep it maintained. Ladies like five o'clock shadows and some like big Grizzly Adams beards and others like clean-shaven faces. I guess the only advice I would have with the mustache, beard or Grizzly Adams look would just be to make sure it's clean. Be sure you don't have your breakfast, lunch, or dinner inside of it and that there are no critters crawling around in it. If you have a mustache trimmer use it and just keep it well trimmed. I have a funny story about this one: I was out with my wife in a bar. One of our local dives. There was some young buck sitting next to me and I was in the middle between him and my beautiful wife.

This guy has the nerve to tell me 'you know, you get more ladies if you shave your mustache and beard" I said "What?" he said "You'll get more ladies if you shave your mustache and beard".

He then told me "Just think about it. Which president has there been that has had a mustache and beard"?

Right off the bat I thought Abraham Lincoln, but it is anything I just thought this guy was a huge tool. I said "Come on you have to be kidding me right?" He begins to tell me how statistics shows that clean-shaven guys get more girls than guys with mustaches and beards. It was so funny how I knocked him off his rocker. I leaned back in my bar stool pointed to my wife and said “Okay I'm here with her. Who the hell are you here with?". This tool was sitting at the bar with nobody on his side telling me how to pick up girls. That would be like me taking income tax advice from Wesley Snipes.

Okay now head to your front door or back door or where ever you keep your shoes at. Are you the type of guy that only has one pair of shoes and they're the blue gym shoes with the two Velcro straps? Okay this is pretty serious guys. As I said before for some reason ladies pay very close attention to your shoes. Maybe it's because they love shopping for their own shoes or maybe it was a gene left inside of them from Eve. Who knows where the hell it came from but it's there. Also if you're out to sell real estate or looking for a business partner they also pay attention to your shoes. So we're looking at the shoes right now.

Do you have attention getters? As in when you're walking they're talking? I think a guy should have three basic pairs of shoes at minimum.

One pair of good gym shoes. Nike, Reebok, New Balance or a good running shoe or court shoe.

I know there are some guys out there that are considered sneaker heads. The sneaker head is someone who collects gym shoes.

There are actually conventions for these sneaker heads and they pay top dollar to keep their collection up as any collector would from Star Wars to classic cars or ladies like with Hugh Hefner. Another pair of shoes you should have are casual shoes, for going out casually. If you don't know what to look for pick up a Maxim magazine or a People magazine or any magazine with movie stars on it. The paparazzi does your homework for you. They always capture the movie stars out in public in their casual attire. Pay attention to what they're wearing so the next time you're out shopping you know what to look for. Finally the third pair I wear is a boot like Lugz, Timberlands or Wolverine. I prefer suede or leather. They actually look really good when you wear some jeans and they're good to wear in the winter. You know that all of this is just tips. You know it's really the person you are that gets the females. Can you hold a conversation? Can you make the ladies laugh? Do you have the balls to go up to them?

All the clothes are is a form of Pea-cocking, come on, I know you've heard that term before.

Think of the male peacock spreading his tail feathers in attempts to attract a female. This is the exact same thing.

Why do you think all of the young bucks by all that GAUDY, flashy crap? The baseball caps with all the flashy emblems on them, the huge flashy belt buckles, the huge gaudy wristwatches with all the flashy stones.

How about on that heavyweight jewelry that's about 5 pounds of lead hanging off their neck. Another form of pea-cocking is driving these cars with the big ass rims.

Makes no sense to me why guys drive around with rims more expensive than the cars they're driving. One guy told me it's the flash effect when he pulls up to a young honey. There you go pea-cocking, it works, it's there and it's one term you should look up.

The easiest way I can explain this to you is to duplicate the attire and the actions of someone famous or someone you know. If you think someone has swagga, look them up and google their pictures. Now don't go become a stalker. Just try to know what they're wearing and how they're carrying themselves. Pick up some magazines and look to see who's wearing what. You don't have to get that exact same name brand, there's still the same kind of clothes with different name brands at regular stores. You're not looking to duplicate somebody's $10,000 wardrobe you're just looking to get an idea of what you should look for. Believe it or not I know quite a few guys that actually shop at thrift stores and also shop the clearance rack.

You know it is really not what you wear it's how you're going to wear it. Make sure your shoulders are back when you walk and be more confident. Don't slouch!

Keep your head up, look at people, smile and say hi when you pass them. They will see your beautiful sparkling smile, check out your new digs (your clothes), get a hint to your new aroma with your kick ass cologne and you say hi and brighten their day.

Try to have some fun making these changes. Do you currently have any lady friends? Coworkers? Anybody other than your mom that you could go shopping with? Ask them to assist you. Ask for their advice. Tell them you're looking to buy a new shirt and tie for a party you have to go to and maybe on their lunch hour they can run and help you pick one out. Now don't go getting all sweaty palms and everything. This isn't a "date" this is a field trip. While you're out with another female other females will see you with a female so they may feel a little safer talking to you. While you're out be a gentleman and always open the door for her and get her opinion on your shirts, ties or cologne. If you get chance, feed her. Tell her to thank her you'd like to take her for dinner and a drink somewhere. Who doesn't know a lady who likes to go shopping? You should easily be able to find someone to go with you and damn it when you're with her "don't sweat the small stuff" "don't go blowing any gaskets" you have to make this non-pressure fun.

When I say don't sweat the small stuff I mean that if you order a cheeseburger and they put of pickle on it and you say no pickles don't go blowing a gasket or make a big scene in front of her. She'll think you're too anal-retentive. Take baby steps if you can't find someone to go shopping with you. While you're out there get the input from all the ladies that are working there.

Whether it's the pants section or the shirt section or the cologne section, there should be a lady in the area working the store. Get her opinion, make small talk and remember practice makes perfect and there is millions of ladies out there to practice on.

Remember the clothes, the shoes and the jewelry are all forms of pea-cocking. If you're out at the club, in the elevator, at the store, or walking down the street pea-cocking is a way to get somebody's attention without saying a word. But while you're pea-cocking make sure your confident and be ready to conquer world.

Teach yourself to talk

This chapter is to be short and sweet because I preached this throughout the whole book. I sincerely feel that people skills are a very important skill in life. Being able talk to people, understand people and just being able to function around people is very important.

Some people don't believe they're born with the gift of gab, but with the desire this can be easily self-taught. One of the leading experts in communication skills is Stephen Covey. This is one guy who you have to look up his books, his audio books and his videos. You can start with "T**he seven habits of highly effective people"**. He teaches how to interact and communicate with other people. Another book or audio to read or listen to is "**How to Win friends and influence people"** by Dale Carnegie. I believe this is one of the most influential books anyone can read. Like I said before if you're driving to and from work or sitting on the train or bus, download it to your iPod or download it to your phone. Just download it to something and use this time to self educate yourself to become the person you really desire to be. One of the speakers that has really changed my life is **Tony Robbins.** In my eyes he is the leader, the number one, yes the head honcho in **Nero-linguistic programming (NLP)** .

If there is something that you want to accomplish or something that you want to change RIGHT NOW, it is a must that you study all of Tony Robbins materials.

You're probably thinking okay this is Rob just trying to up sell all these other peoples materials. But this isn't the case and I have no contracts with any of them, I'm not even linked to them and their websites (YET LOL). These are just people that I have personally studied and they have influenced me and the person I am today. I have preached to you that you have to become a student of who you desire to be, a student of what you want to accomplish in life. Unless you put forth any effort towards your change or what you desire in life it will just be left as a dream.

Now is the time for you to take action! Now it's time to set goals for your dreams and desires to turn into reality! I hope this won't be another course, book or audio that hypes you up for the moment. I truly am writing this book to make an impact on your life.

Sorry there I went off on a tangent. I'm supposed to be teaching you how to talk in this chapter and it sounds like I'm ending the book already. Teach yourself to talk by studying the books I mentioned in previous and this chapter. It's not only getting you out there in daily but also in the real world not just cyber world. You have to get past the fear of talking to people.

You should never have a fear of talking to anybody. You're just talking right?

I mean yea okay have a fear if you have a gun in your pocket and a note in your hand and you're standing in the bank. Yes you should have a fear of talking to somebody if it's to ask for all of the money. Other than that go for it! Really, what's the worst that can happen? Try to become somebody's friend at work (that's if your fear of talking just keeps you to yourself). Try just smiling and saying hi, that should be a small enough baby step to start with. Hi, hello, how are you? There you go, baby steps. If you have a really bad lack of confidence just start with that smile and say hi. Do it enough and then go from there. Talking to someone is easy we just allow fear to make it hard on ourselves. Hence this is another time to reach down grab your pair and say hello.

There are 311,926,523 people in the United States, and 6,953,706,361 people in the world. So if you mess up talking to a couple hundred thousand people you still have pretty good odds of making up for that. If your approach isn't working change it, but how hard is the "hi" approach? I challenge you right now to go out there and talk to 10 people on the street. Smile and say hi to 10 different people. Stop at the store, look for something specific, act like you don't know where it's at and ask the person behind the counter. Make some some kind of joke or some kind of small talk and move on to the next person. Just think in your mind when you talk to the person, that you're a comedian.

Hear that little voice saying "thank you and good night" and keep on practicing.

You have to get over that initial fear and once you have you could say hi and there's no more fear. Try leading the conversation from there, talk about the nice day, ask if they've been following sports whatever team is winning or losing. There's plenty of things for you to talk about you just get nervous and it slips your mind. Don't have anything planned just be natural, be yourself. A little more quirkier version of yourself, but still yourself. Some guys say all you have to do is say hi and make them laugh and you got them. I think for most part it's kind of true, make them laugh and show them a good time.

One good movie to watch is that movie “Hitch” with Will Smith. Man was he one smooth player in that movie, but it was mainly the same thing he got up there and talked with the ladies and made them laugh. You have it in you, we all have it in us, you just have to bring it out. Stop letting that fear control you, allowing fear to control you is limiting your life, your experiences, and your destiny. I wish I could be there to personally help each and every one of you to break down those walls of your comfort zone. I'm hopeful with this book it would be a step in your life, and I'm hoping it to be a huge step in your life, and as your learning with this book I'll still be studying and learning to put out another book. I don't want my books or seminars to just be in vane. I truly wanna make an impact on your life and change it for the better.

I want you to experience all you want to in life and accomplish all you want to in life.

So right now imagine your mouth as the little wind up teeth and I'm sitting here winding them up and about to let them loose so you can run about and talk with anybody that comes in their path. Talk to everybody, say hi to everybody, and study the books that will help you change your life. I can't wait to see you at our gatherings and I know I will not believe with the conversation were having that you were once shy to talk to people.

Short story: This is another short story about another meeting that had my life that can relate to this chapter. Again this is not an improvement chapter, or dream building chapter this is just a chapter to show you what might happen if you just say hi. If you're not interested in it and I'm not offended then jump right past it and move on to the next chapter.

Okay so one day my buddy and I were headed downtown to go to a club. He had the munchies and I had to take a piss so we decided to stop at the downtown McDonald's. We walked in and there was some hot ass Latina in line waiting to order food. There were high school boys elbowing each other to see who could stand in line behind her. And a behind she did have on her! They were standing behind her and they were giddy and giggling still. I open my mouth first “Hey how you doing tonight?”

She replied “Fine” I said “Okay I didn't ask how you looked, I asked how you were doing tonight?” She had a little laugh over that comment.

I asked where she was headed to because me and my buddy were looking for a place to go.

She said actually she was picking up some McDonald’s for her brother and sister and she was staying in tonight. In my mind I was thinking damn this lady is so fine I think she's blowing us off. She ordered her food and stepped to the side. I then placed my order and I wasn't even hungry. But I ordered it just to be able to stand next to her and small talk a little more. Of all times this day McDonald's clerks were on the ball and she had her food in no time and was walking out the door. I was thinking damn I can't let that booty go I mean that girl go. My buddy stepped up to order his food and I followed her out door. I said "Wait I didn't even get your name or your phone number. How am I supposed to take you out on another day?" She started laughing and asked me for my number so I knew this wasn't going anywhere. I figured it was a long shot but I gave her my number and she stored it in her cell phone. We went on with the rest of the night and as usual we had a fucking blast and partied like rock stars.

It was like three days later when I had a call on my cell phone that I didn't recognize so I picked it up and to my fucking surprise it was her. We'll call her Leticia for now. She asked if I remembered her. I mean how can I forget her with a body like that but I kind of downplayed it and said

“Yea weren't you the one we met in McDonald's?” She said “Yeah that was me”.

I asked her if she really had to watch her little brother and sister that night or if she just really did blow me off? She said kind of both.

She already had stuff lined up for that night but she would like to make it up to me. So I say “Great what are you doing tonight? I'm free .”

She says she don't have much time but she'll meet me at another McDonald's. I was like what the fuck? Is she a serial McDonald's person? If she keeps eating McDonald's every day she's gonna lose that little banging body. We set it up and I knew exactly where the McDonald's was that she told me. I head up there and was about 5 minutes late. She was already sitting in her car. I noticed her as I drove by to park my car. By the time I parked she was already standing behind my car. I get out and looked her up and down. Man I could taste that already! Apparently she was feeling the same way. I went to hug her, say hi and kiss her on the cheek but apparently that wasn't enough for her. Immediately she stuck her tongue in my mouth and started making out with me right there in the parking lot. Hell I thought I was being too fast, but this was one fast little momma. I asked her what she wanted to do. I said "You really can't be wanting McDonald's again” and she started laughing. She asked “How far do you live from here?” I was about a 15 minute car ride away. She asked if I had anybody at the place. I told her “I live alone in a apartment.” By now I was thinking man this is too good to be true, this chick is going to set me up, or rob me. Maybe she would have somebody follow us there.

The next phrase out of her mouth was "Let's go to your place and I will follow you". She was so damn fine and I wanted that the first day I saw her.

I had been in this crazy life for some time now and I knew that sometimes a lady just wants to be fucked. I drove straight to my place and she followed me for real. We got out the cars and once again she grabbed me put her arm around my head and started kissing me all over again.

I must admit I was harder than a fucking rock, I wanted to rip her clothes off and throw her on top of a car right there. We finally made it upstairs to my apartment. She didn't even want to see around. As soon as we got up there she threw me on my couch and jumped on my lap and started kissing all over me and freaking sucking on my lower lip. Hell I was going with it. All the way with it! I knew she felt my dick hard as she was riding me with her clothes on. I went straight for her top and took it off with one clean swoop. She had a nice lacy bra and some low-rise jeans. I felt her thong when I interlocked my fingers behind her back. It just turned me on that much more, I brought my hands back up and took her bra right off. She had the most perfect little tits. I didn't know anything about her other than her name. She had to be about 25 or 26. And with this body you could tell she had no kids. She reached down to pull my shirt over my head and threw it to the side. I stood up with her riding me still and flipped her over and put her laying down on the couch. I went down to kiss her again and undid her pants and pulled her thong and her pants off just that quick.

There she was this hot ass fucking Latina with long brown hair about 5'3"and 110 pounds. I went to go take my belt off and pull my pants right off while reaching in my pocket to pull out a condom. Man I couldn't believe this!

She was fucking hot and ready within 5 minutes of us being in my apartment. We're both butt ass naked and I was about to stick my cock in her. There was no foreplay other than the kissing. It didn't seem like she needed any. She just wanted cock in her like now. I was looking around for the cameras. I had to be on the adult version of candid camera.

There is no way that this beautiful ass lady is here now and this isn't some kind of set up. Okay okay stop fucking thinking and start fucking. So there I went. I wasn't going to let it pass me up. If candid camera were filming me I was going to put on a good show. So there we are fucking like rabbits, completely naked fucking missionary style, fucking doggy style, fucking on the massage table, and fucking on the floor. Swear to God this chick knew what she wanted and was multi orgasmic. She fucking convulsed with the first three strokes and it was the same thing about every 10 minutes. We didn't go down on each other, she didn't suck my cock, nor did I lick her clit. All we did was fuck. After about 30 to 45 minutes she abruptly had to go. I was like man sitting in the corner rocking back and forth smoking a cigarette. She said she had a great time, thanks for everything and I should call her again soon. I was like no fucking way, she won't call back again.

Sure enough though like clockwork every two weeks she called and came back. She even sent two of her friends for "massages". That was pretty cool, she opened up and we ran the gamut of every sexual fantasy there was. Later I found out through one of her friends that she was actually engaged. So I was like her boy toy.

No qualms with that on my part I just wish she would've told me so I could have prepared if he ever followed us to a place. See what I get for opening my mouth and saying hi. You never know what you're going to run into once you open up and start talking to people. Don't forget it's a numbers game and put the numbers up on the board player. I'm here for you, we're here for you, don't forget your part of the team now and we will all meet up someday.

MINDSET

This chapter is on mindset which to me is very similar to desire. But maybe that's just in my warped mind. You know you have to have the mindset to do something and accomplish it. But in the same you have to have that desire also, if you have the mindset to do it and not the desire you have slim to none chance that you're going to accomplish it. That's like saying I have the mindset to run 5 miles today but I don't desire to do it. See I have the mindset where I know I should do it, it will benefit me if I do it, but I don't desire to do it. Just like I have the mindset that I want to be successful but today I'm lazy and don't desire it as much as I desired to lay on the couch and watch TV. I have the mindset that I want more ladies in my life, beautiful scantily clad ladies all over my house and apartment waiting on my every need but today I don't desire to talk to anybody, I don't desire to be successful, I don't desire to be a millionaire. See what I mean mindset without the desire is not going to get you anywhere.

So if you don't have the desire yet go back and read the first chapter again. Try and drum up some desire and crystallize it to what you really desire in life and now let's build a mindset for that. When you think of your mindset be sure that you're building a strong one, not one that you let other people control for you. You have to create your mindset and be the controller of your mindset.

I'm going to show you ways that people can put little subliminal bombs into your mindset.

There are many people in life who are like crabs in the barrel. What I mean is a bunch of crabs are in the barrel and a couple of them want to climb out but some of the crabs are grabbing onto them and holding them in the barrel. That's kind of the way it is in life. I hate to say it but there are people, not all of them but there are quite a few, that bask in the failure of others. There are other people out there that don't want to put forth the effort to change their life yet don't want to see you have a better life than them either. So one of the ways they try to hold you back is putting little negative bombs in your subliminal mindset. The bombs might not go off right now but they will be planted in there and your mindset has to be stronger to defuse them and move on.

You can put so many things in other people's minds without them realizing it and you could kind of have a large impact on somebody's day and possibly the future by putting these little negativity bombs in their subliminal mindset. But I do not recommend this. If you are going to put something in somebody's subliminal mindset I suggest you put something positive in there because I strongly believe in karma and if you do not have well wishes for others well wishes will not be returned to you.

Here's the example of how other stuff gets put in your mind, say you're heading out with a bunch of buddies and one of the guys recommends a particular club but you have one of those negative ass doubting Thomas's in the group of guys you hang out with so Mr. doubting Thomas says let's not go to that club because it sucks. Now you may have never been to this club before but already in your mind that club sucks. So next time you're out with a group of guys and they say let's go out and one of them says let's go to that same club you'll say no let's not because I heard that club sucks. Really you just let Mr. doubting Thomas plant something in your mind, a delayed time bomb that just blew up because this particular night Hugh Hefner was going to be at that club with all the Playboy playmates doing a lingerie review. See what you missed by letter Mr. doubting Thomas control your mind.

Or how about when somebody asks you to go get some salt? And you already asked somebody else to get you the salt about 15 minutes earlier and they told you it's not there. So instead of you going to look what's the first thing you say? "I can't find it, it's not there." Instead of going to the shelf that you know your spouse or significant other is going to go to and grab salt that was there all along. Another way of somebody else controlling your mind.

What about when you're out with somebody going to a new environment and they tell you

“Hey keep an eye on your wallet because where we're going these type of people steal”so you go in there have a great time with everybody and when you come out realize that you don't have your wallet.

What is going to be the first thing on your mind? “Those people stole my wallet”instead you forgot you placed it in your jacket pocket. This is another instance of somebody else invading your subliminal mind.

There are many positive ways of influencing somebody else's subliminal mind. When somebody else tells me “Oh I'm starting to get sick” I'm always being supportive and tell them something more positive like “I'm sure it's nothing major just have a cold drink and you'll better.” When somebody tells me reasons why they cannot do something, I say okay now tell me how you're going to do it. Then they start over to say again how they can do it.

This is what you have to do to control your mindset. You choose your emotions, choose to be happy and live life to the fullest. When somebody tries to plant a bomb in your subliminal mind realize what they're doing and say something positive about it and how you're going to achieve or accomplish it anyway. Then turn around and try to plant the positive bomb in their mind.

If it's companionship you're looking for have the mindset that you're going to get to know a little bit about every lady that passes you by in life.

I'm not talking about running up to every single lady you see on the street but every lady you have a chance to converse with. Give yourself chances to converse with them by having the mindset that you're going to get out there into new environments and new experiences to meet your perfect companion.

For companionship a doubting Thomas mindset will kill your chances on meeting anybody. You have to be more confident in controlling your mindset. You know companionship is there for you because I know it's there for you. You just have to talk to enough people and have your mindset that you're going to talk to enough people and have a great desire for that companionship. Close your eyes and imagine yourself right now with your perfect companion, how does she look? What color hair? Can you smell her essence? You have to already imagine yourself with your perfect companion. You have to believe that she is there for you and she's waiting for you to come talk to her.

What about your business mindset? What's holding you back right now? You probably already know. Is it the matter that your mindset is there but your desire is not? How much time in the day are you giving to achieve what you want in the business end? What mindset do you need in your field of business? I mean if your business is a full contact fighter you'll need a different mindset then if your business is a florist. I can't tell you there is one mindset across the board that will work with every different path to be taken in life.

You have to help me here and find out what mindset is needed for you to achieve in your business mindset. My authors mindset is that I not only want to help one person with my book, I want to help 50,000 people with my book. My mindset is I have to get this book out because I know it will affect many people's lives in a more positive way of living their life to the fullest.

So in terms my mindset for this book is as if I have the cure to achieve something great in life and if I don't get it out there I'm not reaching my fullest potential in helping others.

If you find out in your business what mindset helped you to succeed please share that with me and share that with others because I'm sure there's other people out there just like you in business that feel as if they've plateaued yet they know there's something more out there still. If your mindset is that you want to get out there and party like a rock star yet you haven't done anything else in this book then you have the mindset but are still lacking the desire or the **desire** still isn't strong enough. Kind of like the force. The force in you has to be strong enough to control your mindset, to taste your desires and to fulfill your dreams.

Right now choose your mindset, choose your mindset just as you make a choice to be happy. Choosing your mindset is very easy, committing to your mindset is a little harder but with desire it can keep you focused like a tiny little tip of a laser beam until you accomplish what you want.

Then set a new mindset. Find a new desire and go for that. Set up your big dream or goal that you want to achieve or accomplish. Have in your mindset the reasons why you're doing it then break it down in terms of smaller steps for you to achieve what you want and give yourself deadlines to achieve those smaller steps so that you may accomplish it.

So have you chosen your mindset yet? What is it going to be? Really tell me your mindset! Is your mindset in business? That you're going to achieve a certain level?

That you know within 12 months that you will achieve that promotion? You have the mindset and the desire to strive forth on a daily basis and no one is taking that away from you. Have you set your mindset for your companionship that you're going to go out and be that happy-go-lucky person, put that smile on your face, choose to be happy and bring happiness to somebody else's life. You got that mindset to be a total cock in life? That you go out there and be a total asshole to all the ladies because you know nice guys finish last. So you are going to go out three nights a week and get laid as much as you can. Well it's a mindset some people may not agree with it but if that is your mindset fueled with desire you can achieve that also.

There are plenty books on the market about mindset, I recommend you read or download a couple of them to get different points of views.

This is one thing that people who are successful at what ever other endeavors have conquered, the controlling of their mindset.

So once again I tell you you must become the best student there is for the person, the successes, or the endeavors that you would like to achieve or accomplish. I'm hoping this book motivates you enough to keep you striving and learning as much knowledge as you can to become the person you want to be and have the success you want to have.

So before you go to bed tonight or actually when you're laying in bed tonight focus on the laser beam mentality for at least a minute on committing to your new mindset. What do you want your new mindset to be?

What joy and happiness is it going to bring you? How much impact will this new mindset bring into other people's lives? Focus on it tonight, in the morning and throughout the day everyday from this day forward . You control your mindset and live your life to the fullest.

Short Story: Once again gentlemen this is going to be another short story this will be my last short story of this book. But it will not be my last short story because I do intend on writing more books. You can skip this story if it doesn't interest you and just go straight to focusing on setting your mindset.

But this particular story is a story of what may happen to you one day if you reach down grab your pair and speak the hell up.

One day when I was out running the streets (my version of running the streets is out barhopping the clubs) I bumped into an old high school acquaintance.

She was out having a couple drinks with her husband and I really didn't know him from Shynola. We made small talk and she knew me from the old neighborhood and I knew her because all you guys remember when you were that freshman in high school there was that fine ass senior girl that everyone had a crush on. You probably even rubbed one or two off maybe even 10 to 20 taking that cold shower before you went to bed as a freshman thinking about her. Well yeah this time out it was her that I ran into. I was actually surprised she remembered me.

At this time I didn't know anyone else at the club and it appeared they didn't know anyone else either. So we kinda made small talk and caught up but the funny thing is we really had nothing to catch up about.

During the time we met one of my side hustles (business) was selling adult novelties and performing massages for ladies and couple's. I actually had professional business cards made up. I just go with diarrhea at the mouth.

This was an old high school acquaintance but I didn't know if I wanted to even bring it up. Ha ha ha now you know I'm bullshitting I would bring that up every chance I got.

I just didn't want to drop the bomb this early catching up. I bought them a round of drinks and focused on bullshitting with the husband to make him feel more comfortable because he didn't know anybody either.

They went out to dance for a bit and I stood as drink watcher and bullshitted with people around the bar.

We made small talk throughout the night and had a couple drinks together and when I felt the time was right I brought up my side business and handed the husband a business card. It was so funny he was like “no shit my wife can't buy enough toys" she seemed as if she got all embarrassed but she played it off very well. She even asked to see my card and said maybe they will have to stop by someday and see what I have. I know it was just small talk but I did speak up and get another business card out there.

Towards the end of the night they were getting ready to go. I had to tell the husband how beautiful his wife still was and actually told him “You won't believe this but when I was a freshman and she was a senior I had such a crush on her.” She turned all red in the face and was blushing as red as an apple. He was really cool about it.

He didn't know if he should flex his muscles as if I was trying to move in which I really wasn't or just take it as a compliment and move on.

We said our goodbyes and I hugged her and kissed her on the cheek and figured that probably would be the last time I would run into them. About three days later I had a phone call from a number I didn't recognize but I was kind of busy so I didn't answer it and they left a voice mail. When I got time later I checked my voice mails and to my surprise it was her husband calling me.He asked if I could give them a call at my earliest convenience but stated it was not an emergency or important. So I gave him a call back because I was so fucking curious what he wanted. Maybe he wanted to bring his wife over and I'd be able to assist her in selling her some toys.

Well see what the fuck I get for opening my damn mouth. He was inquiring about my massage services. He said that him and his wife were looking for something more adventurous. He felt really comfortable with our conversation and how discrete I was and was wondering if he could set up an appointment to bring his wife by for one of my sensual massages. I was so like no fucking way this is not happening but I was keeping my professional composure and getting a little more insight on how he would like the massage to play out for his wife.

I would normally put some smooth jazz on, light the scented candles, and perform a sensual massage with no shirt on and just a pair shorts, or if the lady or couple was comfortable I'd be totally nude. Normally the couples and some of the ladies would just want me completely nude because they were there for the complete sensual erotic experience.He said he didn't know how comfortable she would be but they did talk about me when they left the club that night and she was flattered and didn't know that I'd had a crush on her. So he recommended that I just do a regular massage with just my shorts on not completely nude. So we set it up for one evening during the week.

I made sure I didn't schedule any other viewings or appointments for this evening because I did not want to give them a rushed experience seeing that this was a first time experience for them. They showed up Wednesday evening at 7pm and I already had the slow jazz playing. The scented candles were burning and a bottle of wine was ready. I figured since this was her first time that she might need something to help her relax. The funny thing is he asked for a beer because he was really nervous. We kind of small talked in my front room as he drank his beer and she sipped on her wine with her luscious lips. After a bit I brought them to the massage room showed them around the toys and made a little bit more small talk.

I always have extra sheets and towels and pillows in the massage room, so I explained to her just undress down to what she is comfortable with and lay face-down on the massage table with her face in a holster that's covered with a fresh towel and put a sheet over her. I told her as she was getting ready that I too had to get ready. I went to go wash my hands with some warm water and I had to have a fucking shot to calm my nerves because I was so excited. As I came back of the room I knocked on the door to see if she was ready.

I always had a extra chair in the room so the husband can sit down and relax and enjoy the show if he didn't choose to participate in his wife's sensual experience. So when I came in the room he was sitting in the chair and she was lying on the massage table with the sheet just covering her midsection and I did notice that she was completely nude.

I asked if she had any troubled areas that she wanted me to focus on before I started. I told her that I was going to take off my shirt to make myself more comfortable if she was okay with that. She was like “Yeah that's fine this way I don't feel like I'm the only one with no clothes on.” My basic massage was more or less like a sensual massage with a little more pressure starting with the back, moving to the shoulders, massaging the neck, going down the arms all the way to the fingers, heading back up the arms then back down the neck all the way to the lower back.

Next I massage the beautiful gluteous maximus then start lightly on the back of the thigh, working down to the calves and then to the feet. I like focusing on the feet not because I'm a foot person, but because every nerve ending in your body is in your foot. So ladies say “Oh I don't like my feet touched” then once you start massaging them either they fall asleep or they start moaning and saying how good it feels.

So I start my basic massage putting the massage oil in my hands first and rubbing them together to get the oil nice and warm before I put my hands on her back. Her skin was nice and smooth just as I had imagined it to be. Her body was flawless, they've never had any kids together both being professionals they never really had the time.

Her hair was nice and long as she moved it over to the side when I started to massage her. Going along I was making small talk with her husband who was sitting on the side and making all kinds of innuendos. As it was about halfway through her massage I asked her husband again if he would like to assist me. This time he got up and said sure he joked if he should take his shirt off also. But she didn't take it as a joke and she said you better. At the time I was massaging her thighs I was on one side of the massage table and he went around to the other. I told them if he'd like he could start up her back right now and I'll finish the legs and feet. So he went up and started massaging her neck.

I was focusing on her thighs and calves he was rubbing her neck and I noticed her hands rubbing his thighs. He was rubbing from her neck all the way down her back and one time he even lifted the towel that was covering her voluptuous ass. So it was really hard for me to concentrate on trying to relax her as I myself was getting worked up. Although she seemed as if she was really enjoying it. Two guys spending the time to focus solely on her and we were there to make her the center of attention.

As I was massaging her feet her husband moved to the side and was massaging her lower back. He actually went from her lower back over her beautiful ass down her outer thigh and moved to her inner thigh with long slow strokes. They both seemed to be getting very much into it and so was I. This last time he was making a circular motion he did not come back up from her inner thigh he started massaging her clit between her legs as she laid on the table.

This was the first time coming to my apartment, let alone my second time seeing them so I didn't know how comfortable they were with me there but apparently very. He inserted his fingers in her and started fingering her starting off slowly and then picked up speed. She was moaning and her midsection started moving up and down off the massage table. She reached off of the massage table and started to rub his midsection.

I moved around to the other side of the table and lightly rubbed my fingers from her ankles, up her calves, on her thighs and to her back. I really didn't get any vibe. They were having some pretty good foreplay going on and I wasn't getting any input so I felt as if I was completed in my work. As I moved my way around to the side her husband moved his way to the bottom of the massage table. He grabbed her by her legs and pulled her down so she was bent over to massage table. He dropped his trousers and started fucking her from behind. As I was leaving the room I told him stay as long as they would like and enjoy their time there. I went to the bathroom to freshen up then to the kitchen for another drink.

They were in there playing for about 15 to 20 more minutes. I didn't mind as I try to provide a comforting, open, sensual good time. Most of my clients are returning clients so I knew they would be back. As I was in the kitchen they were coming out the room him with just pants on, and her with a towel wrapped around her. They asked if they could use the bathroom to freshen up. I said of course and asked if they wanted a beer.

She went to the bathroom first and he came for beer. He told me that as they were there playing she asked him if he minded if she could fuck me. Then he asked me if he would've called me back into the room if I would've.

I told him I'm there to provide a good time for them, and if he would've allowed me to indulge myself in his beautiful wife I would've.

He then told me that he can get her out the bathroom and back on the table right now. I told him no don't worry about it they will be back again and there's always next time. She came out of the bathroom and she was all red and flustered, she said she had really enjoyed herself and couldn't wait to come back. When he came out of the bathroom I walked them to the door. I told them I hoped they had good time and don't be shy to use my number again. I hugged her and kissed her on the cheek, then I went to shake the husband's hand and he put something in my hand when our hands touched. I knew it was a bill of some kind by the feeling of it. I mean I do do this for tips, but I didn't go ahead and open it up with them there. When they left it turned out her husband tipped me out $160.

About 30 minutes later I got a phone call from them, I figured maybe they forgot something but I didn't see anything while I was cleaning the room when they left. It was the husband and he told me they had such an exotic time that they were fucking right now and if I could talk dirty to his wife as they fucked. So I obliged. Hell who wouldn't want to hear her sexy voice moaning for real.

I always say live to fight another day, I didn't jump all over it when her husband was trying to get us back in the room.

I didn't push the envelope as I was in the room because it was their first time there. But this couple was repeat customers time and time again. Me bumping into them was something they had been searching for for some time and they felt comfortable enough with me to allow her wildest desires to come true.

See what may happen if you actually speak up. The more you get out there in life, the more you speak to everybody and have a good time, the more fun in life you're going to have.

In closing

I want to give you all a sincere thank you for allowing me to come into your life in hopes that I have impacted it in some way. Hopefully a positive way and that you and I will strive for success together.

As I mentioned before I'm not the type of person that would say if only I could change one person's life. I want to be the change of hundreds of thousands of people's lives. I want to make an impact, an impact with tangible results. I want to hear from everybody that I have impacted them and how their lives changed. Have they grown from it? Maybe I helped somebody expand their comfort zone. Even something as small as someone being able to have a conversation that they've been too shy to before. That is a way of the small level. Kind of like a baby step in change in someone's life.

This right here is the first book I wrote, the first of many I am hoping. This was a huge step for me to accomplish but it was a big enough burning desire that I had to help change people's lives. I always say some people like me, most people hate me. I bet this book has brought that phrase to the extremes for me. No matter what as I try to tell the people be yourself, maybe a happier more quirkier yourself but be yourself.

This book may seem as if it were kinda short but I tried to pack as much of the knowledge I have into it to make it short and sweet, where there is meat and potatoes for you to read and then get out there and take some action because that's how I am in life. Don't tell me about the labor pains, show me the baby. I don't want to hear all the negativity about anything I want to know your final result and how you came, saw and conquered.

Stay happy my friend since we have to go through life anyways let's live it to the fullest, party like rock stars and have a blast. I'll see you at your party at the top.

Sincerely,
Robert Trevino

www.ingramcontent.com/pod-product-compliance
Ingram Content Group UK Ltd.
Pitfield, Milton Keynes, MK11 3LW, UK
UKHW041935190726
13854UKWH00004B/1595

9 781257 979356